About the Author

Charmian Clift was born in Kiama, New South Wales, on 31 August 1923. She became a journalist on the Melbourne *Argus* newspaper after the war, and in 1947 married novelist and journalist George Johnston.

Early in their marriage they collaborated on three novels: *High Valley* (which won the *Sydney Morning Herald* prize in 1948), *The Big Chariot* and *The Sponge Divers*. Then, in 1954, having lived in London for the previous few years, they took their family to live in the Greek islands. During this period Charmian wrote two accounts of their life there, *Mermaid Singing* and *Peel Me a Lotus*, and two novels, *Honour's Mimic* and *Walk to the Paradise Gardens*.

In 1964 the family returned to Australia and Charmian began writing a weekly newspaper column which quickly gained a wide and devoted readership.

She died in 1969.

Polly Samson is an author, lyricist and a Fellow of the Royal Society of Literature. Her most recent novel, the bestselling *A Theatre for Dreamers*, features Charmian Clift as one of the central characters.

Also by Charmian Clift

Peel Me a Lotus (1959)
Walk to the Paradise Gardens (1960)
Honour's Mimic (1964)
Images in Aspic (1965)
The World of Charmian Clift (1970)
Trouble in Lotus Land (1990)
Being Alone With Oneself (1991)
Charmian Clift Selected Essays (2001)

With George Johnston

High Valley (1949)
The Big Chariot (1953)
The Sea and the Stone (1955,
republished as *The Sponge Divers*, 1956)
The Strong-man from Piraeus (1983)

Mermaid Singing

Charmian Clift

Introduction by Polly Samson

**MUSWELL
PRESS**

Mermaid Singing first published in 1956 by Michael Joseph Ltd

This edition published by Muswell Press in 2021

Copyright © Charmian Clift 1956
Introduction © Copyright Polly Samson 2021
Illustrations by Cedric Flower

Lines from *The Love Song of J. Alfred Prufrock* by TS Eliot
by permission Faber & Faber

A CIP catalogue record for this book
is available from the British Library.

ISBN 9781838110130
eISBN 9781838110154

Additional typesetting by M Rules
Printed and bound by CPI (UK) Ltd, Croydon CR0 4YY

The right of Charmian Clift to be identified as the
author of this work has been asserted in accordance with
the Copyright Amendment (Moral Rights) Act 2000.

MIX
Paper from
responsible sources
FSC
www.fsc.org
FSC® C020471

5 7 9 10 8 6 4

For my mother
Amy Lila Clift

Mermaid Singing by Charmian Clift

In the winter of 1954 writers Charmian Clift and George Johnston left London, with their children, to live by their wits and their typewriters on a Greek island. Kalymnos, one of the Dodecanese – the dozen dry islands scattered along the coast of Turkey, like the fragments of a Greek plate smashed in an international domestic – would not have been their first choice. Stony and rough though it was, the couple needed a story and Kalymnos offered an extraordinary and tragic one. It was an island almost entirely dependent on its sponge fishing fleets. A population of fourteen thousand people relied on just a few brave men, divers who risked their lives fishing for sponges off the coast of Africa for seven months of each year. There was little other industry (mass tourism hadn't yet been invented) and the popularity of synthetic sponges was killing the market for real ones and impoverishing the island.

Already celebrated back home in Australia (where their first collaborative novel had won the prestigious *Sydney Morning Herald* prize), Clift and Johnston had been in London for four years, part of a diaspora of Australasian talent that enriched the cultural life of the fifties and sixties. They had published a couple of collaborative novels to good reviews, taken tea at Faber's offices with T.S. Eliot. They lived in a flat provided by George Johnston's employers, in a red brick mansion opposite the

Russian Embassy in Bayswater. Their London friends numbered many artists, Sidney Nolan, Colin Colahan and Cedric Flowers among them. They drank cocktails with Peter Finch, Laurence Olivier and Joe Orton and bashed away at their typewriters late into the night.

George Johnston had become dispirited working on Fleet Street. One of Australia's star war reporters, he had trotted the globe, walked with Ghandi beside the Ganges, met the Dalai Lama, witnessed the Japanese surrender ceremony from a ship and was one of the first to visit Hiroshima in the aftermath of the atom bomb. The work he was being asked to write and wire back to Australia was increasingly tittle-tattle about the royal family or the size of filmstars' breasts. Clift was frustrated too: it was a period in which she later described herself as feeling she was losing her identity. There wasn't a scrap of time for her own writing. She was backstopping with the children and researching at the British Museum Reading Room, dashing down notes for the books that she and George wrote together once he got home. Late at night, if she glanced out of the tall window, across the dark shadows she'd see the outlines of all the trees in Kensington Gardens that her children were not allowed to climb. She writes of George Johnston needing Benzedrine to stay awake, barbiturates to sleep, and 'the inexorably circling fingers of a thousand clocks spinning our lives away'. Princess Margaret was on the front pages, smog hung around. Charmian Clift was a year past thirty to her husband's forty-two when they threw it all in for their Greek island. Their children Martin and Shane were seven and five.

The yearned-for catalyst to escape was a BBC documentary about a scheme to take the island's unemployed sponge divers to Darwin to revive the ailing pearl industry there. Their families would join them later. For a novel that would feature bravery and macho divers – and set on the yearned-for Mediterranean island – it would also be a story of emigration.

Unfortunately the pearl-diving scheme was abandoned shortly before the family were due to leave London. 'But I've already cancelled the winter coal so we'll have to go!' Charmian Clift insisted they go through with it.

She tells us she thinks of her children as 'hostages' as the plane takes flight from London's 'guernsey cow coloured' skies to Athens. Her voice is immediately engaging, the guilty word 'hostages' arresting. Caught bang in the middle of the awkward hinterland between Simone de Beauvoir and Germaine Greer, her thoughts about children and the role of their mothers remain at once strange and relatable.

Ovid describes how it was while flying over the honey-rich island of Kalymnos that Icarus found confidence in his wings, and 'began to rejoice in his bold flight.' For Charmian Clift too, as noted by her insightful biographer, Nadia Wheatley, it was on Kalymnos that her writing took off. Once the novel about the sponge divers was out of the way, written mainly by George Johnston, and with gusto – 'Roll over Hemingway!' she wrote to friends Pat and Cedric Flower at the start of the year, she was able to find a portion of time. Unshackled from collaboration, her own words found their form. It was a tricky metamorphosis, according to Cedric Flower, who was staying with them for part of the year (and whose drawings grace each chapter head) who claimed that George Johnston rankled when she fought off his suggestions to make her writing more colourful or catchy.

Life on the island is tough. It's honey-days are done. Outside her window the rhythms and traditions seem almost medieval. The sight of a crippled young diver, his legs twisted from the pressure of the deep, makes her weep and wish to leave. The island's children are starving and the onus for survival falls heavily on God. Her style is immersive, she brings us with her into glimmering rooms, to orthodox ceremonies and rituals that are rooted in paganism. She's writing events as they happen, with fresh, thrilled eyes that take in the important small details and are not blind to darkness. She is fascinated by the position of the island women, and women generally, notes at a Kalymnian wedding that the bride is 'still padded around the cheeks with puppy fat,' and compares marriage to human sacrifice.

Her thoughts about her own children always strike a reverberating note. One night, for instance, a macabre youth runs along the waterfront 'wearing only a lace curtain topped by a German helmet', and afterwards she worries, as she watches them play and fly kites, that they are 'only pretending to be normal.'

There's ecstasy later as she glories in the children's freedom, and her own. She wears trousers to the Tavernas and drinks with the men despite that it's an island where even lipstick or sitting in a café exposes a girl to 'moral danger'; best of all she insists on writing her own book.

She often deploys acid wit. She compares the swaggering divers and their kombouli to the patriarchy she's left behind and the Old Etonians flicking their keychains. Charmian Clift was a bold feminist, years ahead of her time, and reading her two memoirs, and the volumes of her weekly newspaper essays from the sixties, it is often astonishing to remember that she was writing before the birth of the women's liberation movement. In *Mermaid Singing* she says of her own marriage: 'all embracing cooperation is the only workable arrangement. But I have the faint gnawing suspicion that there will come a time when I will somehow find myself several paces in the rear, watching the flick of his keychain and quite unable to catch up because of the weight of the baggage I am carrying.'

Her imagery is indelible: the slaughterhouse blood with its ruby gleam, the slaughtered pet lambs curled whole into earthenware pots, Irini's entire set of stainless-steel teeth 'giving the impression that the silver icon above the bedpost had made a pronouncement', the baby being raised from the font dripping with wine and oil, Sevasti with a face by Donatello, scampering about the mountainside, miraculous in her red petticoat.

The voice is warm and intimate, testament to the fact that at times the book seemed to be writing itself in the form of letters to friends or in the pages of her journals.

She's open to every experience, delights in the language, the food, the people, nature, the sea. She becomes exuberant in the sun, mesmerising, her descriptions take flight. This, on the ancient village of Chorio, is hypnotic. 'Everything is painted blue from the merest brightening of stark white, like a blue-rinsed sheet, to a thick, rich ultramarine. Stairs melt into walls, corners curve, pavements swell into domed ovens. Sometimes there is no line of demarcation between house and sky and walls soar up and thin out into purest atmosphere or the sky sweeps down to your feet, solidified, with two pink windows and a pot of red carnations drawn on. The black-clad women are exclamation points against the blue ... Every scrap of colour sings – a boy's red jersey, an orange cat, a tray of poison-coloured sweets, a flower dropped on a twisted stair.'

We all know what happened to Icarus and it's hard not to let his shadow fall on these pages or to dwell on Charmian Clift's tragic death just fourteen years after they were written. Better to think of her here on Kalymnos, sitting at her typewriter in the window of the tall, narrow yellow house that still stands on the waterfront. The year is 1955 and she's writing to the Flowers:

'Building ivory castles like mad. Very, very happy. Even if it all fails will never be sorry we got away from it all for a bit, anyway. Love, Charm.'

Polly Samson 2021

Mermaid Singing

I have heard the mermaids singing, each to each.
I do not think that they will sing to me.

T S Eliot, *The Love Song of J Alfred Prufrock*

I

We came to the island of Kalymnos in the small grey caique *Angellico*, belting in around Point Cali with a sirocco screaming in from the south-west, a black patched triangle of sail thrumming over our heads, and a cargo of turkeys, tangerines, earthenware water jars, market baskets, and the inevitable old black-shawled women who form part of the furnishings of all Aegean caiques.

It seemed to be a fine brave way of making an arrival.

'Mother of God!' gasped an old lady between vomits. 'The little ones! Look at them! They do not understand!'

'Bah, old grandmother!' The curly-headed deck hand flung the contents of a bucket into a mountainous green wall of water rearing over us. 'They are sailors, the children. Sailors! Anyone can see.'

The wave hit. The benches went crashing from one side of the deckhouse to the other.

'Grrrp!' said the old lady in a strange strangled way and clutched at air. The curly-headed boy steadied himself nonchalantly against the splintered door frame and obligingly hauled in the bucket at the end of its rope. The 'little ones,' who belong to me, emerged dripping from a convulsed heap of turkeys, benches, cardboard suitcases, broken pottery, market baskets, and upended old ladies, with their small fists full of tangerines and their small faces crimson with ecstasy.

Obviously this was beating the Battersea Pleasure Gardens hands down.

'*Mum!* Why does it come up all yellow and lumpy?' (Martin is seven and has a scientific turn of mind.)

'Because she didn't chew her breakfast nicely nor swaller.' (Shane is fourteen months younger, and female.)

The deck hand dragged the old woman across to the door as if she were a wet bundle of rags and pushed her head into the bucket. 'You see, old grandmother,' he said contemptuously, holding her poor bedraggled old head down, '*sailors!*'

Our lean friend and self-appointed guide, Manolis, who had been shot across the deck in a crouching attitude, now rose from all-fours with a dignity I greatly admired, and, turning to George and me, said with the air of a patriarch who had brought his tribe to the promised land: 'My brother and my sister, we come now to Kalymnos.'

And so, indeed, we did.

There, heaving ponderously above the peaking wave-crests, were gaunt grey mountains, slashed and scarred with sulphurous fissures and streaming ragged clouds. And at the foot of the mountains was a town, an improbable town that from across the wild sea had the appearance of carefully arranged coloured matchboxes — a doll's town to amuse a child on a wet afternoon. Beyond the little cubes of white and blue and yellow ochre a hill rose out of a valley with a ruined wall and three round towers; and below the houses a forest of matchstick masts tossed on what would ultimately prove, no doubt, to be a nursery bowl filled with water from the bathroom tap.

The *Angellico* kicked and shuddered and bounded forward with a final sickening lurch down into the swirling sea. Then, unbelievably, it was sliding in around the breakwater on an even keel, and the sodden old women crossed themselves and began to sort out their bundles with good-natured equanimity. We slid in to a little wharf alongside an ugly customs building and three houses that had been stolen from a Christopher Wood painting.

The children were handed ashore like heroes, engulfed in admiration. It was as well, on the whole, that neither George nor I had enough Greek to explain that they had been heavily laced with drammamine before leaving Kos. I have a theory that sailors are made, not born, and the products of the biochemical laboratories are a better insurance policy than bunches of herbs or tangerine peel, or even, I suspect, the desperate supplications of St Nicholas which are the background accompaniment to Aegean travel. I was not to know until some days later that two passengers on the caique from Vathy had been washed overboard that morning and all the deck cargo lost, although at the time it surprised me a little that Manolis should cross himself so fervently the minute his feet were on dry land again.

'Brav!' he said admiringly to the children, and to us. 'That damn *Angellico*! It'll turn over next trip. You see!'

Only two hours before, at Kos, with the sea fretting and fuming outside the harbour all the way across to Turkey and the fishing boats scudding in to land under taut orange sails, it had been this same Manolis who had urged us aboard the *Angellico*, which was rolling and dipping even then inside the sheltering wall of the castle.

'*Po-po-po-po po!* Nothing! Nothing!' he had said, indicating the sea, the shredding sky, the orange specks of sails fanning out urgently from Bodrum. 'You come to Kalymnos now. Very good island. Very good people.' And he had helped us aboard the *Angellico* as if it had been the *Semiramis* leaving Piraeus for a summer cruise. 'You see now,' he had said, as he skilfully dislodged two old women from their seats to make room for us.

'Today at Kalymnos I find you one good house. You don't come back no more to Kos.'

I suppose it is indicative only of his complete amiability that a Greek will always tell you what you want to believe. Now Manolis had crossed from Kos to Kalymnos a hundred times and was perfectly well aware that it was a dangerous day and certainly no day to put to sea with two small children in tow. His nonchalant minimising of the risks was activated entirely by his knowledge that we wanted desperately to get to Kalymnos and we hoped for a calm crossing. I am sure he would have been deeply wounded had anyone suggested he might have shown

7

greater concern for our welfare by advising us against sailing. 'But this was the day they *wanted* to go.'

His behaviour has continued consistent. Manolis is pliable. We have found ourselves picnicking in a hailstorm on his assurance that it was bound to turn out a beautiful day. We have wasted many expectant hours waiting for events and people and information that have never materialised. The bus has left the station. The ship, alas, weighed anchor two hours ago. The party is not tonight, it was held last week. If either of us expresses a wish (often, indeed, we have no need to express it; Manolis merely assumes that we will) he instantly assures us of its imminent gratification, not from any conviction but from a sincere desire that things may turn out as we hope. He sees nothing illogical in this. It is his expression of friendship.

Looking back on it now I think it was probably only the greatest stroke of good luck that we *did* find a house in Kalymnos, and that within half an hour of our arrival, exactly as Manolis had predicted in Kos.

It was a spindly yellow house on the waterfront, with a little cast-iron balcony overhanging the *plateia* and four staring windows that looked down the broad harbour road with its row of coffee-houses under the ragged casuarina trees and across to the small coloured cubes piled higgledy-piggledy at the base of the mountain. We inspected it with the owner, a stout, effusive woman who wore a blue coat and skirt and the sunglasses that here are a symbol of class distinction and accordingly are worn also at night or when the sun is heavily overcast.

Our inspecting entourage consisted of Manolis, two slim shy young men in working clothes whom he introduced as his nephews, a gnome-faced engineer named Mike who had worked in the United States and spoke English, the wife of the proprietor of the adjoining coffee-house, and about a score of ragged snot-nosed children, part of the shrill horde of hundreds who had followed us along the waterfront and were now crowded into the room, choked up the tunnel of the stairs, or waited in the *plateia* below for further developments.

There were four bare rooms with pale, streaky, limewashed walls and an improbable number of double doors carved with tricky lozenges and painted white. There was a large white kitchen with a red stone floor and two tiny open grates of whitewashed brick behind a flowered curtain drawn across the gigantic chimney. There was, as I had been warned, no bathroom, and the lavatory was as noisome as I had expected, but at least it was separate from the kitchen and there was a cistern above it, lacking a chain.

Could the landlady, we asked, have a chain attached to the cistern?

Why, certainly, certainly! Nothing could be simpler. The matter would be attended to tomorrow. Anything we wanted! Anything!

The rent was set at six hundred *drachmae* a month, and this figure was discussed and debated by everybody in the room, including the ragged children, who carried the information to the crowded stairway, from which point it was borne to the patient crowd in the *plateia*. There, I gather, it was considered at length, as well it might have been for it was daylight robbery. However, we had no way of knowing this at the time, being fools with money generally and coming fresh from London rents.

'Is that cheap enough, Manolis?' asked George.

'My dear brother!' said Manolis, who had evidently observed from our slightly desperate expressions that we *hoped* the rent was set at a fair figure.

If we agreed to pay such a sum could the landlady provide the necessary sheets and blankets for the beds, cupboards for hanging clothes, cutlery and table linen, cooking utensils for the kitchen.

Everything! Everything! The best she owned would be at our disposal. It would be her first concern that we should be as comfortable as if we were in our own home and the little darlinks happy.

The little darlinks were by this time prancing up and down the blue tunnel that led from the street wearing their silliest expressions and shrieking abuse at each other to the wonderment

9

of their wide-eyed audience of Kalymnian children. For a moment, shamefully conscious as I was of the contrast between the plump, well-fed, warmly-dressed and odiously-behaved little darlinks and the grave wonder of the scantily clad and undernourished children who regarded them with such soft, shy glances, I would gladly have disowned my two. But as I grasped one small hand firmly in each of mine I realised that their hands were hot and damp, and the two pairs of blue eyes turned stubbornly away from mine were filled with strain and uncertainty.

Martin's lower lip began to tremble. His fingers tightened convulsively. Shane, always alert for a cue, took the deep shuddering breath that always heralds a bellow.

'Oh, it's *awful,* Mum!' Martin sobbed. 'I haven't had any peanut butter since London and I don't know what *anyone* is saying.'

Obviously they had had about as much as they could bear. And who could blame them? For the last two weeks they, who had always lived a life as snug and safe and ordered as a comfortable income, a comfortable home, and loving parents could provide, had been hauled on and off aeroplanes, Aegean ships, smelly caiques, in and out of hotels and *pensiones*; they had been asked to eat lukewarm squid slithering in olive oil, cold macaroni, bread without butter, boiled goat's milk which turned them up: instead of the paradise of sunshine, blue skies, and sweet little donkeys which they had been promised they had spent miserable hours perched tiredly on top of mounds of baggage in bleak terminals and on rainswept wharves. They were cold and unhappy and homesick. I felt for them with all my heart. For so, suddenly, was I.

'Tell her we'll take the house.' It didn't matter if the rent was too high or the house damp or the attic infested with rats. We had come to a point where we had to stop and sort ourselves out.

It was only then that I noticed that the tap above the kitchen sink was attached to a little tank of painted tin that had no sign of pipes leading into it.

'But where does the water come from?' I asked.

Not far. Nothing. A mere five minutes' walk. I would find a public tap in the street behind the corner coffee-house, and of course there were the wells. I could get myself an old kerosene tin. If I did not care to fetch the water myself there was a very nice woman who would be glad of employment. She would carry the water, clean the floors, do our laundry very cheaply and cleanly. Would I care to interview her in the morning?

'My dear sister!' Manolis muttered fiercely, 'don't let yourself be cheated! The daughter of my sister, who sells very fine clean vegetables in the small shop at the corner, will fetch your water and clean your clothes for far less money. This woman is only trying to find employment for a relation!'

'We can leave that until later,' I said. 'What interests me at the moment is this question of water. If there is no running water I take it the cistern doesn't work?'

Manolis shrugged.

'But what is the point of having a chain attached to an empty cistern?'

The landlady beamed and spread her arms wide. It was what I had asked for. Her one object in life was to oblige me and to make the little darlinks happy.

In the bare front room the sobbing was dying down, and through the hiccoughs I could hear George's voice, '... and those big schooners over by the lighthouse are called *depositos*. You see, they carry all the food for the sponge divers to eat, because they are away from home each year for a long time, six or seven months ...'

'Would *they* carry peanut butter, do you think?'

2

'Eh, Mister George, what you fellers goin' to do here?'

'Write a book, Mike, as we told you.'

'Yeah, but …' American Mike's wizened little face was cocked sideways. He looked more than ever like a sceptical monkey. His crooked brown hands were busy with a tasselled *kombolloi* of big amber beads.

'But what, Mike.'

'Well, that's what I tellum, Mister George. I say to them, these fellers is writin' a book about Kalymnos. But plenty of people here say to me, Manolis says how you can write the permit for goin' to Australia. Manolis says no trouble for you to fixum. Plenty fellers here think you and Mister Charmian is a committee, somethin' like that.'

George, wearing the phrenetic expression that was becoming habitual, explained all over again that we were not a committee, that we didn't know any committee, that we had no influence whatever with the powers who arranged migration or selected migrants.

A crippled old man who seemed to be the town-crier was at this moment hobbling past bawling an announcement of the imminent arrival of the *Kyklades* from Piraeus and the expected departure of the *Andros* next morning for Rhodes.

He left the shipping schedule in the air and came over to the table under the trees to listen. Three sponge-divers at the next table pulled their chairs closer. The inevitable circle of children closed in, though doubtless they, like the sponge-divers, the town-crier, and American Mike, had heard it all before. By this time the whole town had heard our explanation — and nobody believed a word of it.

I still found it a little difficult to believe myself. For many years George, like other journalists, had grizzled fairly constantly about the nature of his work and sworn in his cups, like other journalists, that one bloody day he would just go off and live on an island and write books. (For a journalist in his cups the alternative earthly paradise to an island is a pig farm. There is some mysterious affinity between a journalist and a Berkshire sow that to me is completely unfathomable, but then I married into the island persuasion of journalists. I heard once of a newspaperman who actually did give up a lucrative job for the fatal allure of Berkshire sows, but, alas, I could never find out what happened to him eventually. Remembering Mr Tasker's Gods, I suspect the worst. I also know another journalist of neither pig nor island persuasion, a truly original fellow who rustled up fifty pounds from his friends and went into the real estate business. *He* became filthy rich in no time.)

Well then, about a month previously George had been despairing in the classic journalist vein about the treadmill of Fleet Street and the impossibility of writing anything worth while when your only time for creative writing was at night and then you were too drunk or too tired, and how when you reached forty your future was calculable and you felt that with every Princess Margaret Surprise and every Foreign Office Sensation you were hammering another bar into place around your cage, and now the bars had become so close and numerous that you couldn't see out any longer or remember how the sky looked or whether there was anybody left in the world who walked free.

There was nothing unusual in all this. It was true, and we had long known it and long accepted it as the price to be paid for the nice flat and the car and the good schools for the children and the first-class tickets for yearly holidays on the Continent, and the rounds of theatres and concerts and entertaining and the pleasures of good food and good wine. Perhaps the extraordinary real and horrible sensation of suffocation we had both felt that night was due to nothing more than the fog, which had crept through the long windows and was wreathed in the curtains and hanging like gauze about the candle flames. Outside in the Bayswater Road the night was the colour of a guernsey cow, and on the pavements the leaves lay in a sad yellow pulp, mulched by all those homeward-plodding boots. Why should it be, suddenly, a thing too infinitely depressing to be borne that the women were already wearing snowboots and those shapeless gruel-coloured overcoats that would fill the streets for the next six or seven months? Why should one weep because the salt was too damp to pour? Perhaps if at that moment I had refrained from the masochistic urge which compelled me to get out the box of colour slides we had taken on our springtime holiday in Greece ... the little islands floating magically on an indigo sea, the cypresses stiff against early morning oyster skies, the pink domes, soaring saffron shafts of column, the three donkeys on a hill at noonday, wading through crimson flowers ... Perhaps if that very day we had not met, by accident, a friend newly returned from Greece who had asked me to come into the B.B.C. to hear a radio feature he had made on the sponge-diving island of Kalymnos ...

It burst like a star, so simple and brilliant and beautiful that for the moment we could only stare at each other in wonder. Why the devil shouldn't we just *go*?

So we did.

We had no means of communication other than sign language, and we had a bank account that didn't bear thinking about. Still, we thought we might be able to last for a year if we managed very carefully and stayed healthy. We had for some years published a novel every year or so, not very successfully, but we thought that it might be just possible to live by our writing when our capital ran out.

Kalymnos seemed a good place to go because there was a story there that was interesting which we could get to work on straight away as an insurance policy against the next year. If it didn't work out ...

But of course it would. Once the decision was made it was impossible, it was beyond the bounds of reason, that it should not work out.

'You are a pair of romantic babies,' said a friend of ours. 'And of course you'll live to regret this folly. On the other hand I believe that although the mermaids are mute it is necessary for everybody, once in his life, to go down to the sea and wait and listen.'

'Hey, Mum! *Mum!*' Martin whispered urgently in my ear, his blue eyes amazed with hope and on his mouth the little deprecating smile of the disenchanted. 'Does he really mean *mermaids?* Or is it just grown-up talk? Are there mermaids in Greece too, besides the donkeys and the longest sausages in the world?'

'Silly,' Shane said sleepily, 'there are mermaids everywhere.'

'Oh, *I* know they're not true,' said Martin quickly, with the lordliness of disappointment. 'Excepting perhaps for a *rare* one. Mum, might there still be a rare one?'

Ah, but how to say to American Mike under the casuarina tree that we were looking for a mermaid? How to explain that we were civilisation sick, asphalt and television sick, that we had lost our beginnings and felt a sort of hollow that we had not been able to fill up with material success. We had come to Kalymnos to seek a source, or a wonder, or a sign, to be reassured in our humanity.

'Well, you see Mister George, it seems funny to these fellers here, all these fellers here don't want nothin' but to get away from Kalymnos. They all want to get to Australia. They don't want for to have to go on divin' for sponges. Ain't nothin' here but sponges, Mister George.'

We told Mike that we had both come from Australia originally.

'Yeah, I know, Mister George. Manolis he tellum that. He tellum you can write the permit.'

We began all over again.

'Well, if you can't write the permit, maybe you could let one of these fellers live in your house when he gets there.'

But we don't have a house there.

Where is your house then? Is your house in England?

We don't have a house. We have no house anywhere in the world. Our house is this yellow one we rented yesterday for as long as we can pay the rent.

And now I know that this is something a Greek will never understand. For we are the new nomads, the twentieth century, who wander the earth with trailing roots, our possessions portable, our dwellings temporary. Not for us the parish register, the crammed attic, great-grandmother's furniture, the field planted out for the next generation, the family vault and the ancestral worms. We pay weekly for the space we take up in the world, from the moment we open our eyes in the hospital ward to the time we close them in the rented house.

American Mike was making intricate double flips with his *kombolloi*. The three divers were smiling at us encouragingly. A little barefooted girl had crept up behind me to touch the stuff of my skirt.

'O.K., Mister George,' Mike said finally, and grinned. 'You just tell any feller here anything you want. He'll fetch it.'

I had the feeling that we had scraped through an important test.

3

Kalymnos declared itself only gradually. On first impression it seems to be a much larger place than it actually is, partly because the massiveness of the rugged mountains that encircle the town like an imprisoning wall has the look of belonging to a *big* landscape, partly because the activity of the caique-filled harbour and the constant bustle along the broad and crowded waterfront street create an air of business which by Aegean standards is almost metropolitan.

Looking down from our balcony it was not difficult to believe that this was one of the most active working ports of the Aegean. It was far less credible that the spectacular cliffs rising sheer from the sea were not, after all, the ramparts of a continent but only the overdramatic edges of an island merely ten miles long and, at its broadest point, less than five miles wide. And it was not until much later that one came to realise the appalling emptiness that lies behind that surrounding wall of rock — the bleak and stony uplands, lichened and lonely, where no tree will ever grow and where even the thin, harsh vegetation of the stones must struggle for survival.

Around the anchored caiques the seagulls quarrel querulously, but high in the air over a huge scarred crag that overhangs the town a lonely eagle hangs on stiff pinions like a scratch in the sky. Beyond the crowded coffee-houses nothing exists. From below the balcony comes the soft clicking of the gamblers' strings of yellow beads. It is a soothing, idle sound, and behind it hangs an eternal silence.

It is hard to believe now that this was once an island of forests and rivers, of shady groves and glens. Except of thorns there is not a thicket left, for the centuries of occupation by the Turks deforested the island with the ruthlessness of a locust plague. It is impossible to guess how many people lived here before that occupation, but at the beginning of this century there was a population of thirty thousand dwelling contentedly, peaceably and prosperously. Today the population is fewer than fourteen thousand, and while the fecundity of Kalymnian wives is something to marvel at, the depopulation of the island continues at an alarming rate. Today its young men are fleeing Kalymnos at the rate of hundreds every year. Within a generation it is easily conceivable that everything will have come to an end. The island will be dead, virtually uninhabited, a victim of this most devastating of all centuries.

It is only the sponge fleet, already under sentence of death from the synthetics, that holds the old pattern together, preserving it for a little time longer in a state of tortured survival, only the maiming, terrible life of the divers that postpones for a brief period — five years? ten? twenty? … it can hardly be longer — the doom that is certain.

It is an island under sentence, an island in suspense.

I can remember that the day after George and I had heard our friend's radio programme in the B.B.C. studios my neighbour Jo and I had taken the children, hers and mine, across the Bayswater Road to seize the few faint fugitive gleams of autumn sunlight filtering through the gold drift of the leaves. We had sat on a rug spread across the damp grass of Kensington Gardens while I talked about Kalymnos and about our plans for going there.

Sheep were cropping down the hill that dips to the Serpentine, and there were curls of blue smoke rising from the heaps of burning leaves. Over by the Round Pond three elderly gentlemen in hacking jackets and wading boots messed about with the rigging of their model boats. A tiny foetal-faced woman with the staring, startled eyes of a lemur under her headscarf scudded through the doomed elms behind the straining leashes of three slavering boxers wearing studded collars and rugs of Hunting Stewart tartan. And along the swept paths the nannies passed and repassed in brisk, well-shod pairs, erect and determined behind the high, well-sprung caravels that contained the pink and chubby heirs to England, taking the air before a nourishing nursery tea.

There was Jo's young blunt face with the wide hazel eyes fixed attentively on mine; behind her were the two pretty babies in their good leggings and coats sharing rusks and marmite sandwiches on a fur rug spread beside the high black pram, Shane's small figure, squat and square in her duffle coat, busily trundling her dolls backwards and forwards along the path, Martin under the chestnuts, boredly gathering conkers.

Was there really somewhere a hot, high rock where no trees grew, where children were hungry, where men were forced to pluck a bitter living from the bottom of the sea? Or was it only in my head, the shape of it, the barren stones that the sea circled, the fear and desolation? The day before, a black disc had spun its calculated revolutions in the soundproof cellar of the B.B.C. among the switches and dials and red bulbs, and Kalymnos had been *there* for half an hour, its harshness tearing through the silky, soothing narration.

Among the reds and golds and the drifting smoke of a familiar London afternoon I was haunted by crippled men in seamen's caps, by shrill sad voices of singing girls.

The crippled men never walk in pairs. That is the first thing you notice. They wrench their ways alone among the streets and coffee tables by the sea or limp stubbornly between the strong. There is something queer and furtive and angry in this avoidance of the other crippled men, something almost of jealousy, as if in the terrible equal marks of suffering there lies an unbearable resented proof of an equal intimacy with that cruel and passionate mistress who has rejected them but holds them yet. *I Thalassa!* The sea! The sea!

No one seems to know exactly how many crippled divers there are in this strange town. Three hundred, says one. A thousand, says another. But every year the sea sends back eight or ten or fifteen more, paralysed by the great blue pressures of the deep and silent places under the ocean.

There is something terrifying in this mastery of the sea over the men. The bold or the cautious, the young or the grizzled, it is all the same. They dive shallow and they dive deep, some protected by rubber suits and copper helmets, some wearing a strange devilish costume of black tights and bodice and weird mask, some naked as the day they were born, their hands clutching a huge stone to carry them down. They have theories and systems to outwit the pressures. They have candles burning to Saints Stephanos, Nikolas, Mikailis, Georgios, Demetrios. The sea doesn't care. If she can't kill them, or doesn't choose to, she will probably bend one of their legs just a little to show who has command of the situation. And afterwards they too can limp through the twisting streets with a cropped-haired boy behind to carry the basket of fish they must sell, or six eggs in a handkerchief and a little bag of gambling numbers stuffed into the armpit where the police won't find it … a *drachma* a dip, only a *drachma* and fine fresh eggs …

We know many of them now, the crippled men, from old Emmanuele Manglis, the doyen of divers, who was paralysed late in life — and in a dive any boy in his first lesson could have made — to eighteen-year-old Panorimides Katapoulis, who was paralysed a few weeks after our arrival, on the last dive of the last day of his first cruise.

Panorimides comes from a family of divers (his father was drowned diving off Cyprus three years ago), which means a large family, although the family of Panorimides, with eight brothers and three sisters, is larger than most. Now, until the other boys become old enough, only one brother, Themoli, will be able to go away diving.

From the balcony of our yellow house we saw Panorimides taking his first walk since he left hospital. He came all the way down the broad street that separates the coffee-houses from the harbour with his brother Themoli on one side of him and another lad in a seaman's cap on the other. The curved stick dangled over his arm, because he couldn't quite get the hang of it yet. Instead he grasped his brother's arm, and when they came below our balcony we could see Themoli's arm shaking with the pressure of that angry white-knuckled hand and the dumb ferocity in the eyes of Panorimides as he tried to force the useless trailing leg to move.

They turned him around under our balcony, awkwardly and gently, and the three of them walked back the way they had come. It took them fifteen minutes to get as far as the war memorial, but they walked right in the centre of the street and they looked neither right nor left nor gave a single greeting to the strollers who watched their progress interestedly. I stood at the window and wept until long after they had disappeared from sight, the two straight boys in the black divers' caps and the twisted boy propped between them, the boy who didn't wear a diver's cap any longer. That was one of the few times I thought I would have to go away from Kalymnos.

The other thing you notice about the crippled men is that they cannot keep away from the sea. In the upper reaches of the town, where the majority of them live because it is the poorer quarter, the houses are small and bright and cosy and you can grasp your neighbour's hand across the windows. There are no streets, only the loose mountain boulders and scoured fissures of clay and cracked mountain soil to walk on, with a rough step or two hacked out from the rocks in the really precipitous places. But down they come, heaving and stumbling and clutching at walls and doors and boulders for support, making their painful progress to the sea. During the day you find them at the coffee tables on the waterfront, always on the waterfront, selling fish or the soft herb-wrapped cheeses of Kalymnos, or oranges or cigarettes or peanuts. At night they limp among the harbour *tavernas*, and occasionally they put down their trays and drink a beaker or two of *retzina* with the men who still wear black caps and have two sound legs tucked under the table, the men who drink and gamble all winter long and sometimes spill a furtive libation on the floor before they raise their glasses … a libation to what, I wonder?

Once in the dusk I saw a man with a stick leaning on the harbour railing looking at the sea. Behind him a bald boy squatted beside a basket of soggy squid, idly torturing a couple of crabs. A thin woman wearing a patched print dress and a clean white headscarf stood silent at his elbow. He was a tall man with strong shoulders and a fine grey head, and he leaned there on the railings for an hour or more just looking at the sea. I am sure he did not see the caiques coming in or the caiques going out, or the *Dodecanissos* chugging in from Symi to berth by the long pier where the men with the handcarts waited. It was the sea he was looking at, only the sea — as if by looking long enough and quietly, with eyes that no longer harboured anger nor bitterness nor even resignation, he might at last find the answer to it all.

'Well, I've got my papers,' said the freckle-faced twenty-year-old who had joined us at the café table. 'They'll send a telegram when I have to go up to Piraeus. In five weeks or so I'll be off to Australia.'

'You're really happy about it?' George asked.

'Well,' he said matter-of-factly, 'I'm glad it was settled before I signed up for another season's diving. There are better ways of making a living. This diving, it's not a good life.'

The crippled diver Dionyssos was limping down through the tables garishly hung with little sandals and children's clothes and tablecloths and women's pullovers on wooden hangers, crying the merits of a new shop opened in the narrow street beside Agios Christos.

The freckled boy turned his head away and drained the little cup of coffee in a gulp, and in doing so he brushed my cigarette case off the table. I bent to retrieve it, and under the concealing table I saw that his legs were moving reassuringly, one against the other.

4

As a writer's observation post the yellow house could not have been more strategically situated. The masts of the anchored *aktaramathes* — the graceful Kalymnian diving boats — seemed to lean on our windows. We awakened each morning to sea sounds and sea smells and white-framed pictures of boats and mountain and cloud and sky. Water reflections rippled on our high, white, lozenged ceiling. And across the *plateia* beneath our balcony all of Kalymnos passed each day as if for review: captains and divers, sponge buyers and sponge sellers, deck hands and fishermen, strolling to the coffee-houses and *tavernas* and gambling tables past the idle winter-harboured boats; their busy wives, heavy-skirted, black-coifed like medieval women, swooping across the *plateia* with water pitchers, market baskets, strings of fish, bundles of faggots or wood shavings from the carpenters' shops, flat boards stacked with new-baked bread; strangely garbed men from the mountains herding ragged, skinny sheep to the slaughterhouse; barefooted children playing endless complicated games with stones and sticks and little piles of almonds; labourers straining at the ropes of the great clumsy two-wheeled *carros* laden with flour or wood or drums of petrol or crates of sponges; street vendors shrilly crying the merits of edible commodities the names of which sounded much more exotic than they really were — *oktopothes! smarithes! pastelia!*

baklava! portokalia! psaria freska! maroolia! fistikia zesta!
frash-elaikia! yaouti! galatobouriko!

The ground floor of our house was a sponge-clipping room
where twenty men with great black shears sat all day long half-
buried in the soft salt-smelling piles of yellow sponges, clipping
and shaping them round and smooth.[1] Without moving from
the house at all we could observe a complete cross-section of
Kalymnian activities, all the movement of the harbour, the
main street, the several houses diagonally opposite and the
innumerable coffee-houses, *tavernas*, shops and bakeries behind
the row of salt trees.

To say that we were unconscious of all this, or ungrateful
for it, would not be true. But as this is going to be rather in the
nature of a chapter of difficulties, I must first state categorically
that from the moment we arrived in Kalymnos we knew that
it exceeded all our expectations. Never, not even in the most
abysmal depths of our miseries, did we pine to exchange our
arid rock for one of the gentler islands where the lotus grows.
No lotus, nor indeed very much of anything else, grows on
Kalymnos.

In fact it was apparent from the very first that the good
people who had so fervently impressed upon us the primitive
nature of Kalymnian living conditions had been dead right! If it
was not quite the backside of the universe, as George asserted in
a moment of profound despair, it was understandable from the
very nature of our first preoccupations that he should be led to
this conclusion. For the landlady, after stowing the first month's
rent in an enormous imitation crocodile handbag and kissing the
little darlinks profusely, had departed on a tidal wave of effusive
bonhomie without remembering to tell us that it was not only the
cistern that was unfunctional.

We had made the discovery of the lavatory's basic
uselessness within five minutes of realising that two of the

---

1   There is a symbolic significance in the fact that it has since become a coffee-
     house, another of the innumerable *kafeneions*, which, in Kalymnos, are the
     waiting rooms for idle men.

rooms were uninhabitable. It had rained very heavily in the night (the sun-drenched travel posters that lure tourists to the Aegean take no cognisance of December) and our baggage, piled haphazardly into an empty room pending the arrival of the promised cupboards, was now completely sodden. Muddy cascades were still jetting through a broken skylight and several separate fissures in the ceiling. Another bare chamber, euphemistically described as 'the dining-room,' was in a state even more apocalyptic. A widening lake in which some fragments of sponges symbolically floated surrounded the rickety deal table and four frail chairs placed precisely in the centre of the room, and little rivulets crept across the landing and dripped drearily over the stairs. Great blotches of dampness had begun to ooze through the thick stone walls, and each time I passed through the room I expected to find evil fungoid growths forming. It was, moreover, bitterly cold.

We had all slept in our clothes overnight — not just a normal quota of clothes, but layer upon layer of clothes — huddled under overcoats on the hard iron bedframes because the blankets could not be delivered to us until the next day. By this time we were stiff and aching in the backs and shoulders and a little desperate besides with trying to rid the house of the hundreds of interested children who had been swarming at the doors and stair railings since dawn. There were bald-headed boys with cigarette trays and boys with baskets of peanuts and boys with trays of buns and honey cakes and little dark-eyed girls with matted hair and bare brown feet who had already captured Martin and Shane and were passing them around delightedly. My desperation was in no way diminished by the odious smirkings on the faces of my children nor by my observing them stuffing into their pockets the marbles and dried figs and peanuts and half-chewed *caramellos* and even *drachma* pieces that were being pressed upon them.

I also realised with some astonishment that three women with water jars were quarrelling vociferously in the kitchen, while a fourth was gathering up and bundling into a sheet the sodden clothing we had snatched from the waterlogged cases in the spare room. All four wore identical full black skirts, checked aprons and black headscarves, but while the three in the kitchen were immensely fat and indescribably noisy, the one in the spare room was very thin and silent. While the three black-draped behemoths argued and gesticulated and appealed to me, to George, to the assembled children and to heaven, she just went on gathering up the clothes, clucking quietly to herself as she examined each damaged garment.

'Oh, my God!' said George and grabbed a cigarette boy out of the horde in the passage-way. '*Manolis!* Do you understand? *Manolis!*' George, I realised, was suddenly conscious of a phenomenon that was to become recurrently more impressive: that Manolis was always there when he was not wanted and never there when he was. 'Manolis!' he repeated, with wildly rolling eyes.

The boy grinned and sucked his cheeks into hollows and pinched his mouth in until only one tooth pressed against his bottom lip. He hunched his shoulders, and one hand gesticulated grandly with all the fingers splayed. It was wickedly clever, and bursts of giggling exploded down the stairs.

'Yes,' said George tiredly, moving two chairs to the edge of the lake. We sat down and waited. There did not seem to be much else we could do.

After a time the thin woman came from the spare room and closed the door quietly on the depressing spectacle of our private Atlantis. She placed the sheeted bundle of clothing in the passageway and went briskly into the kitchen, reappearing a moment later with the water jar on her shoulder. She nodded to us briefly and calmly descended the stairs, cuffing a quiet way through the children. The three other ladies descended after her, but wrathfully, with swishing skirts and shoulders indignantly set back. They went down the stairs and out of our sight like old galleons sinking. They took their water jars with them.

Within five minutes Manolis came with the two shy nephews deferentially walking two paces in the rear. Mike the engineer slouched after them. The children closed in behind. We proceeded in a solemn file to the lavatory.

'My dear brother and sister,' Manolis said with a dismissive shrug. 'This is nothing. Nothing! All the same here.'

'It does not work,' George said quietly. 'Nothing works.'

'*Po-po-po-po-po!*' muttered the taller of the two nephews, in accents of awe, his right hand circling reverently in front of his chest. '*Afto ine poli pallio!*'

'Mr John he say now this thing is very old,' Manolis translated. 'A very old article. But it is nothing, my brother and sister. All the same here.'

'*Po-po-po po-po!*' said Mr John, looking at us with commiserating chestnut eyes.

'Mr John he say more better you get a new one.'

'Then why didn't Mr John say so yesterday, when the bloody landlady was here?'

Questioned angrily by Manolis, who treated both young men as if they were small recalcitrant children, Mr John spread his hands wide. His eyes were mournful, but his mouth twitched slightly.

'*Dropee,*' he murmured.

'Bah!' snarled Manolis, raising a hand as if to strike him. 'He say now he is shy.'

The other nephew, a small, graceful man with thickly lashed, shy brown eyes and beautiful delicate-looking hands, said something softly.

'Mr Michael he say you not asked them yesterday. If you ask them they tell you quick this is no good.' Manolis thoughtfully considered the odious object for a minute, holding up one hand for silence, then he said: 'My dear brother and sister, more better you get a new one. I think so.'

'Jesus, Manolaichi! What they want to go spending *their* money for?' Mike the engineer — later to be distinguished as American Mike — winked at us broadly, screwing up his little wizened face like a sardonic monkey. 'That *gorgona* she's getting plenty enough rent from these fellers. You go tell *her* buy a new one!'

Manolis shrugged helplessly. '*Dropee,*' he said.

A small boy on the stairs, a small boy with some foul-smelling white paste rubbed into his shaven bullet head as a discouragement to lice and two candles of mucus suspended from his nostrils, volunteered the information that the landlady had taken that morning's ship to Rhodes. She hadn't, said another. She had gone to her sister's house at Vathy, over the mountain. Or was it to the village of Choria, two miles inland from the town?

'Christ Almighty!' said American Mike and ordered Snotnose to go and find out, and be smart about it. The house was locked, said the child, panting back a few minutes later, the candles longer than ever. There was nobody there.

'My dear brother and sister,' Manolis said sagely. 'I do not think you see this woman for a long time.'

It was his second accurate prophecy. We did not, in fact, see her until the next month's rent was due, by which time our difficulties had been to some extent overcome. That they were overcome to any degree at all was entirely attributable to the friendly interest of American Mike, who, though he had long since abandoned the attempt to keep up the standards of Gary, Indiana, still remembered with a sort of cynical nostalgia that he had once lived in a world where things were arranged differently.

He puzzled it out with his cloth cap pushed back and his fingers scratching abstractedly at his wiry grey hair. Then, 'Yah! Yah!' he said, his small blue eyes snapping with illumination. 'I get it now. Don't you worry no more. I fix him up real good.'

What's more he did, even to such ultimate refinements as a covered bin with a lid that said *Bon Ton Cheese Corn, An Appetising Snack* and a bunch of sweet-smelling bay leaves to hang from the ceiling.

This aroused in the breast of Manolis a frenzy of jealousy. More better, he said darkly, to heed the advice of Mr John and get a new one. That Mr John's advice did prove sound in the long run did nothing to detract from the pioneering achievement of American Mike in these first rounds of what was to be a long and bitter struggle with the sanitation of Kalymnos.

'These damn Greeks!' said Mike imperiously. 'They don't know nothin' about hygiene!'

The sister of the landlady, wearing identical sunglasses and carrying an identical bag, appeared miraculously when Mike had completed his tasteful arrangements. She was led firmly on a tour of inspection. She brimmed with full heart. Had her sister not promised we would be as comfortable as if we were in our own home? Everything was at our disposal. Everything!

Then could she please give us some more cutlery to supplement the few pieces that had been sent with her nephew? I opened the kitchen drawer, brushed away the few mice droppings that had gathered in the night and begged her to witness. There were three rusty knives (one with the metal handle stamped *U.S. Army*, another with a blade compounded not of steel but of some curious elastic substance that bent at a touch), two forks (one of which, by the loss of two of its three prongs, had become a sort of skewer) and two jet-black teaspoons which had obviously been dropped into a hot fire at some time and not retrieved for several days — not retrieved, possibly, until our arrival gave them a revivified value! A solitary cracked plate rested on the bottom row of four empty plate rails, a single battered saucepan stood on the chimney piece, a forlorn relic of richer culinary days. There were two glass tumblers and a rather nice earthenware *liyinei* with one handle missing.

Manolis, of course, had once more exhibited his genius at vanishing at the first breath of trouble, and I was obliged to make out as best I could. I am forced to the conclusion that Lillian Gish was a great, a consummate artist. I mimed as if my life depended on it, I contorted my face into a gamut of emotions, ranging all the way from anguish to polite surprise. I never succeeded in arousing the least flicker of comprehension in my audience.

I led her by the hand into the bedroom and, taking one of the thin coarsely woven blankets between my fingers, I shuddered violently. Spasms wrenched me. My teeth chattered. It was an act for which no rehearsals were needed. There were only two meagrely thin blankets for each bed, and George and I were still sleeping in all our clothes, wrapped in our overcoats so that the children, at least, might be spared pneumonia.

'Brrrrr!' I rumbled exaggeratedly through rattling teeth.

'*Darlinks!*' She had the same articulation and passion for our children as her sister. Tenderly, she clasped them to her bosom. Obviously she grieved for them from the bottom of her heart, not because they were cold, but because their mother was mad.

Equally futile were my endeavours to explain to her that the hanging space her sister had provided was quite inadequate. The promised cupboards had never arrived (it was months later before I realised they never would) but the nephew had brought six bamboo pegs, arranged on a sort of wiggly lattice frame, which he banged up quite haphazardly and very high on the plaster wall. Things could not be *hung* on the bamboo pegs, they had to be *thrown*, but since the nails would not hold in the plaster, anyway, and the whole contraption fell down every time we attempted to use it, its technical shortcomings were the least of our worries. Our outer garments were strung around on chairs and door knobs. And those awful suitcases were still stacked on the floor, unpacked.

The arresting spectacle of the submerged floor, studded with soggy hillocks of sponges like a relief map of the islands of the Aegean, left her equally unperturbed. The varied and cheerful chorus of water pinging and dripping and gurgling down from the roof into assorted dishes, buckets and old tin cans which helpful neighbours had dispersed around the house at the moister strategic points, must have sounded like music to her ears, since her smile became, if anything, more beatific.

After she had gone Manolis appeared. I suspect he had been hiding around the corner watching for her departure. 'My dear sister,' he said calmly, 'you worry too much. The winter is soon past here. When the weather is good again Mr John will mend your roof.'

(With the arrival of spring and the ending of the rains Mr John did mend our roof. For all I know he mended it beautifully. There will be no more rain on it to test his workmanship until next winter, and by then we shall be gone. When the weather was warm we received our additional blankets too. Presumably the landlady no longer needed them. By then we had no need for them either. At the present moment they are folded neatly on top of the unpacked suitcases in the spare room.)

Now Manolis was only voicing the Aegean philosophy of *then pirasi* or *avrio*, which is the same as *mañana*, only rather more Greek, being, I suppose, the ultimate corruption of the classical and more complex Epicureanism. One adopts it eventually through sheer necessity — and a very pleasant philosophy it is too. But it takes a little time to see the wisdom of it, and at first I was balanced so precariously between laughter and tears that the most I could do was to hold on tight and somehow save myself from toppling into real hysteria. It wasn't time yet for philosophy.

We were still strung tight, I suppose, by the tensions of the last few months. And behind the last few months stretched all the nervous years of pace without rest, of struggle without fulfilment, of taxicabs and telephones and the inexorably circling fingers of a thousand clocks spinning our lives away. It is harder to slow down than you think. I worried too much, and continued to worry too much, for a long time yet, even though Manolis' philosophy was early proved to be sound.

For though the landlady never really equipped our house, the cheerful curious throngs of women who trooped in and out of the rooms, prying and chattering and exclaiming, apparently took it upon themselves to supply what was lacking in the way of necessities for household management.

'What does she want, Manolis?' I asked when the first one came and set down on the table before me two forks and a minute and very beautiful silver spoon resting in the folds of a clean, pressed dishcloth.

'Why, my dear sister, this woman looked in the drawer of your kitchen this morning and was ashamed that you had so little. She would not wish you to think that all the women of this island are the same as that rich one who does not even give you what you pay for. She would like you to do her the honour of using her forks and the small spoon that belonged to her great-grandmother.'

They came all that week — one with a saucepan, another with an embroidered tablecloth, another with a blue-bordered plate and a huge china chamber pot decorated with green roses.

They came with drying cloths and sponges for the floor and cups without saucers and saucers without cups and graters and spoons and cooking pots.

'My dear sister, this woman says that she hopes you will be happy here ...' '... she is ashamed that she has only this plate to offer you ...' '... this woman weeps because you are a stranger and she is afraid you are lonely ...' '... a few eggs for the children and a jar of tomato preserves ...'

'But I *can't*, Manolis,' I wailed. 'They're all so poor. They haven't enough for themselves.'

'Take. Take, my dear sister. Or they will think that their things are not good enough and be ashamed. Take. It will give great happiness.'

Perhaps after all it is more blessed to receive than to give. It was my first Kalymnian lesson in humility.

And then there was Sevasti.

Sevasti, you might say, simply happened. In no sense did we ever employ her. It was rather that, by a process of time, we acquired her.

In the beginning she was just another figure among the scores who thronged happily and unselfconsciously through our house by day and by night. During our first weeks, when we lived as swamp dwellers, it was not at all unusual for us to sit down to meals under the interested observation of a dozen women and children who jostled in the doorway or stood laughing and chattering behind our chairs. I still remember with a shudder the nightmarish unreality of waking, shivering in the damp grey dawn, and looking directly into a little grinning face whose nostrils ran thick yellow mucus.

During this period there were, as I have explained, the four women with their water jars, three of them fat, and one of them very thin. Sevasti was the thin one. Every morning they proceeded solemnly to the kitchen, where they set down their jars and began to wrangle away furiously. The nature of their daily argument was clear enough, but since the finer points of their claims were lost on me and since they provided a welcome distraction for the rest of my uninvited guests, who crowded eagerly into the kitchen to advise, exhort, agree or disclaim, I was inclined to leave them to it and, with St Dominic, allow God to judge the right.

Unlike the stout trio, Sevasti never wrangled or wasted time in voicing her claims or merits. On the second morning she appeared with the bundle of clothes she had taken away the day before. It had rained solidly all day and night, and the clothes, although beautifully laundered, were slightly damp. She conveyed to me by signs that she had ironed them as dry as she could. This seemed sufficiently miraculous to me, but the three stout competitors instantly appealed for witnesses to testify that they could do the laundry infinitely better, could do it *dry*. Unperturbed, Sevasti took the red water jar from the kitchen and came back in a few minutes with it filled with sweet drinking water. Two small boys followed after, one with a kerosene tin filled with well water for the dishes, the other proudly bearing a bucket of sea water for the lavatory.

This done, Sevasti took the covers from the beds, shook them over the stairs, folded them neatly and turned the mattresses. While the other three ladies in hoarse asides were telling each other what a slovenly way this was to do the beds, Sevasti had her skirt hitched up over an old red petticoat that flapped about her lean shanks and was down on all fours sopping up the flooded rooms with a handful of sponges. On the third morning she produced from an unsuspected but capacious pocket in that same red petticoat a handful of nails, and with a stone she found in the kitchen she banged them up in a row along a wooden rail in the hallway and hung our coats neatly.

On the fourth morning the cornucopian pocket of the red petticoat contained a bundle of strong string and, again using the stone for a hammer, she rigged a line four thicknesses strong from one side of the spare room to the other, well above the tide mark. Within a few minutes dresses and jackets and shirts were out of the cases and on hangers strung across the room.

On the fifth morning, by this process of quiet attrition, she had completely worn out her competitors. They departed still protesting, their jars on their shoulders, their merits unproved. Sevasti was in possession.

She has possessed us ever since. For the miserable little sum of fifty *drachmae* weekly — and no fifteen shillings has ever been spent more rewardingly — Sevasti is ours and we are Sevasti's. And being Sevasti's we are also the possessions of her children, Fotini and Irini, who are handsome, Maria who is not, Georgia who is still at *gymnasium* and clever as well as handsome and little Georgios who entered the world like a belated recompense only to find his name bestowed already on the last of the long series of female disappointments. Sevasti, overjoyed, had called him Georgios, anyway.

I think Donatello would have liked to carve Sevasti, cutting the lines deep in her thin face and tilting her head so that the leathery folds of her cheek emphasised the beautiful modelling of her thin fine nose and the flat plane of her brow. Her smile, for all the broken stumps of teeth and spaces of shiny pink gum, is enchanting, her hands truly marvellous. And in spite of the marks of obvious suffering — a pattern in flesh of the looting of her home by the Germans, its ultimate destruction by British bombs, the near-starvation and flight to Turkey, the nomad life of a refugee in Palestine and Egypt — in spite of an inherent gentleness that is calm and lovely, Sevasti carries within her an inextinguishable spark of raffishness. It is apparent in the very way she wears her coif, not folded severely about brow and chin like the other women's, but rather loose and slipping on top, with ends always coming untied and flapping around her shoulders. It is the raffishness that leads her to dispose of the empty tins of the household in a mad hurling game played from the balcony, with George as her partner and harbour buoys, caiques, and even passing pedestrians as targets. She breaks the handles of cups and the edges of plates at the rate of three or four a week.

But when Sevasti is out on the mountains, freed temporarily from the problems of an incurably sick husband, four undowried daughters and her own obsession to give each of her five children *education*, she is like someone reprieved. She bounds over the rocks with her skirt flapping and the ends of her coif streaming out behind her. She snatches at flowers, herbs, unripe fruit and ears of green wheat as though she might never see such things again. I have the irresistible feeling that no mountain is high enough for her, not even the far bleak cone where the church of Elias the Prophet is perched like a little white dropping from heaven. On the mountains Sevasti is in flight, at one with the herb-scented wind and the belled black goats and the wild high arabesques of the darting flocks of swallows.

Once, much later, in the still, sunny convent that stands among the olive trees over the mountains from Chorio, in the placid valley of Argos, Sevasti said: 'This is what I should like life to be.'

We were sitting together, the four of us — George and I, our friend Yanni, and Sevasti — in the pretty room of Sister Karsiani, a nun of perhaps thirty years who has that breathtaking beauty of tranquillity which the convent life so often gives a woman, perhaps in compensation. A young novice had just taken away the coffee cups and the high white bowls from which we had eaten the delicate creamy yoghurt made by the sisters in the convent dairy. It was siesta time and Sister Karsiani had made for the children a bed with pink-striped sheets and handwoven blankets laid over wonderful pale striped rugs on the high railed-in wooden bedshelf that is the most charming feature of true Kalymnian architecture. When the children were curled up she had poured cold water over our hands from a white jug patterned with silver-grey leaves and dried them on a soft towel and bade us rest a while before we began the long walk back to Chorio.

The children slept and it was very quiet in the little room. The embroideries we had been examining were heaped vividly on the table in the centre of the room, but everything else was pale and cool and still. A shaft of early afternoon sunlight filtered through the leaves of the loquat tree and queerly illuminated the eye of some long-dead *archimandrite* surveying us with bearded remoteness from a bleak black frame high on the white wall. Occasionally we looked up to see a wimpled nun startlingly silhouetted in the sunny oblong of the doorway, smiling at us.

Sevasti lay on the bedshelf beside the children's mattress, her toes curled over to hide the holes in the feet of her stockings, one gnarled hand automatically patting the nearest small hump in the blankets.

This sudden remark of hers and the wistfulness of it startled me deeply, for in the stillness and paleness of the room my thoughts had been running uneasily along the channel of convent life too. But it wasn't of the cool pretty cells set about the whitewashed courtyard I was thinking, nor the paths among the flowers, the cheerful thud of wooden looms, bright flick of needles, wholesome dairy smells under the dark vaulting, fresh-turned earth among the olives and the hoes laid down — nor even of the great dark well of curved cyclopean blocks and the bits of pagan marble built into the chapel walls. I was thinking of the neat whitewashed cellar under the chapel, with the charnel pit of bones in the middle and of tranquil Sister Karsiani giggling herself into hiccoughs as she pulled aside a pair of gauze curtains to expose a shelf of polished skulls.

'This is what I should like life to be,' said Sevasti. 'A little room like this, so clean and quiet, and every day to kneel with God among the gold and flowers. Each day quiet work; each night quiet sleep.'

But do they bury the bodies first? I wondered distractedly, and *dig them up again*? Or — the horror of it! — do they chop off the heads and throw the rest into the pit?

'If my man was only dead and I had no boy,' Sevasti went on, 'I would come tomorrow with my girls and we would each put on the habit and go into our little rooms and —'

'Your *girls*!' Yanni had been dozing, head in hand, in the corner of the room. He sat up straight, his eyes wide with horror, and I thought for a second that he would voice my thoughts concerning the shelf of skulls. But it was the flesh over the bones that was worrying him. 'Your *girls*!' he repeated furiously. 'Are you mad, Sevasti? It's all very well for you; you're an old woman. (Sevasti is forty-five.) But those *koritzia* of yours, they need a good strong man apiece. Fine healthy girls like that! Do you want to kill them? Better you took a knife to them than shut them up *here* for all their lives! You take a good look at all these nuns. Sick! Every one of them. Sick! No man, no baby inside her, a woman gets sick. It isn't natural for a woman to pray all day. By God, I'd rather marry my Yanoula to the garbage collector than lock her up in Argos!'

His vehemence quite shattered Sevasti's thoughts of serenity. She was erect and stiff on the bedshelf, and her leathery cheeks were wet with sudden tears.

'Blah Blah! Blah! Big mouth Yanni! What do you know about marriage? What does any man know about marriage? Your lot only have the fun of putting the babies into us. You don't have to bring them out, or feed them, or weep over them, or fold their hands when they die for want of two hundred *drachmae* for a doctor! How do *you* know what a woman wants? Marriage is slavery, that's what marriage is. It's a broken back and a broken heart and work from morning until night. And not even a decent sleep,' she added wryly, mopping at her face with the back of her sleeve, 'because either there's a baby crying or that big strong man you think we all want is busy putting another one into you. I've had thirty years of it. I know. There's no end to the pain of it, there's no rest in it.'

(I am reporting this conversation as if I had clearly understood every word. In fact I suppose that even at that time my Greek was still at the stage of a few nouns and phrases and a handful of verbs I understood only in the present tense, and conversations were conducted with bits of Greek, bits of English, grimaces, gesticulations, and goodwill. But it is true that with people you love there is a wealth of understanding, of communication and response, that transcends the difficulties of language. Sevasti and Yanni in Sister Karsiani's room at Argos were as bitter and violent in their viewpoints as a man and woman anywhere in the world, in any language, and I understood them as well as if they were speaking in the careful English of the public schools.)

'Well,' Yanni broke in, rather taken aback and inclined to be conciliatory, 'you've had bad luck. If your husband hadn't got sick you'd be living in fine style now, with a grown-up family and good dowries for your girls. But how do you know it's going to be like that for them? Is it right to deprive them of the chance of finding out for themselves?'

'It's going to be just the same for them,' said Sevasti bitterly. 'Because they haven't a dowry between them. What man is going to take one of them without a house or money or a stick of furniture? Do you think I want to see my pretty clever girls married to some fourth-rate diver who'll take one of them only because no girl with a decent dowry would look at him and he needs a slave around the house? I'll lock them up in Argos or send them to the ends of the earth first!'

'That big mouth Yanni!' she muttered fiercely to me as we scrambled up the stony path through the sparse mountain fields. Yanni, unburdened by baskets or by children, was fifty yards ahead of us, free as the air, leaping along the twisting trail with the agility of a goat, his dark handsome head thrown back, his green shirt billowing. The full sweet strains of his song drifted back: '*Ella! Ella!* Come! Come! Leave your father and your mother ...'

'And where's *his* wife?' Sevasti added angrily. 'I know where. Over the washtubs! She's not jumping around the mountain with four babies in the house. After four babies you can't jump much, anyway. It hurts. *Leave your father and your mother* — bah! It's better to be a nun at Argos.'

Yet for all her wistful longings I don't really think Sevasti's small neat skull will ever grin from the shelf in the white-washed cellar. Convent life isn't for her. I have too vivid a recollection of her at the christening party of her niece's first child — a Hogarthian figure transferred from the steel engraving of *Gin Lane* to the scented lamplight of the Aegean, her coif dangling from one ear and a wickered flagon of *retzina* poised high, sloshing the glasses full, her own enormous tumbler beating time to the *bouzoukia* rhythm. (It is not uncharacteristic of Sevasti that on this occasion she inexplicably managed to get the *petrello* and *retzina* bottles mixed, so that for days afterwards all the guests stank of kerosene.)

I have so many pictures of her — wry, sardonic, passionate, gentle, raffish, sad. But alive, every one of them, warm and breathing and alive. I can see her now, hanging like a pterodactyl in the upper branches of a nut tree, stealing green almonds for Martin, shinning over the wall of the richest garden in Kalymnos to find vineleaves for the *dolmadhes* and plunging back in a whirl of red petticoat, boxing Fotini's beautiful ears as though Fotini were still a little girl.

Sevasti loves life too much ever to retreat from it. She loves laughter and bawdy stories and her own sardonic little jests. (Every day for two weeks she allowed George to set the fire in the kitchen grate, ironically watching him as he laboriously split kindling wood and fumbled in the charcoal bin. Then she quietly pushed him aside, soaked a bit of sponge in paraffin, set it alight in the grate, had the fire blazing in ten seconds and wordlessly went back to her dishes.) She loves the interminable squabbles in the kitchen with Yanni. She loves to play with the children as if she were still a child herself.

All Greeks are fond of children. Our most constant parental problem is to prevent our two from being hopelessly indulged. But Sevasti carries her affection for Martin and Shane to the point where her protectiveness is fierce and fanatical and her solicitude as tender as if they were her own.

On that inevitable and horrifying day when we discovered that the children's heads were crawling with lice it was Sevasti who soothed us and Sevasti who crouched over them for hours, combing the eggs out and dousing them in kerosene. When Shane one morning appeared with a bright yellow face and ochreous eyes it was Sevasti who murmured, 'Ah, *chrisophea!* That's nothing!' and Sevasti who organised a doctor, who supervised Shane's diet and took her temperature with more enthusiasm than accuracy. And it was Sevasti who warded off the horde of old women in black who stormed the house with long kitchen knives, anxious to work their own cures on my poor yellow child.

For some reason that is still a mystery to me all Kalymnian children contract jaundice at some time or other. The local cure is to cut the child's forehead with a knife or razor blade into a lattice of cuts 'to let the evil worm out,' and then to slap a thick garlic poultice over the raw wound. Lots of the children carry their crosshatching of white scars for years, like a tribal marking.

Sevasti's staunch stand for doctors and modern pharmaceutics surprised me a great deal when I finally realised what the old ladies with the knives were wanting, because Sevasti herself is as full of herblore and magic potions as Old Mother Shipton. It wasn't until later that I realised she had turned her back on all her own deeply held convictions simply because she couldn't bear to see Shane hurt. The knife cure was not really necessary for children, she explained guiltily, if you had the money to spend on a doctor and medicines. But it was of no use to call a doctor if an adult caught the complaint. Then only the knife would serve.

'If you catch the worm from the child,' she said to George, 'I will cut it out myself. Like this —' snicking away in the air with the kitchen carving knife — 'poof! Nothing. Two days you are better again.'

George turned quite pale, and even after Shane's recovery he kept out of Sevasti's way. I often observed him examining his eyes carefully in the little mirror in the kitchen, and more than once he remarked carelessly that his complexion *always* tended to be sallow.

Shane, with the aid of a strict diet and the drugs designated by the local doctor, recovered in a week, quite unscarred. When Martin's attack came some time later the system was established. The old ladies kept their kitchen knives for peeling vegetables and slitting open fish, Martin sailed blithely through his illness in five days flat on a tide of prescribed medicaments, and Sevasti, with a reformer's zeal, had long Hippocratic harangues with the old women in black who sat with their earthenware pitchers around the public well.

'Sevasti's all right,' Yanni says grudgingly, 'but she needs a little *mathema* — a lesson — every now and then. She doesn't know her place. Do you know that one day when we were all at Argos — you remember that day — she asked *me* to go and fetch water!'

'Well,' I murmur unwarily, 'what's so awful about that?'

'What's so —' Yanni is bereft of words. His hands pluck at the air, his chestnut eyes roll heavenward, he sketches a despairing cross on his tattered shirtfront. '*Paithi mou!* My child! Am I or am I not a man?'

'Yes, but if I asked you to get water you'd fetch it for me, wouldn't you?'

'That's different. You're a lady.'

'Isn't Sevasti?'

'*Paithi mou,*' he explains with injured patience, 'Sevasti is a servant. Is it right for your servant to ask your friends to carry water?'

Now I am on delicate ground. Sevasti is a woman of some education and background. In another society she would be a gentlewoman in reduced circumstances. Yanni is a poor and practically illiterate carpenter. Although I suppose Sevasti is in some sense our servant, since we give her a little money each month, she is much more than that. She is the household prop and stay without which our whole tottering domestic edifice would collapse. I deeply admire her courage and fortitude, respect her opinions on a good many subjects and pay her that deference due an older woman of charm and character.

But Yanni is also a household prop — Manolis' nephew, shy Mr John, who came first to our house at Manolis' command and afterwards because he liked us. Slim, shy, chestnut-eyed Mr John, whom we one day found ourselves calling by his Greek name, Yanni, a change of address that seemed inexplicably to change his whole character. Or perhaps by that time we were beginning to rely on him. Like Sevasti, he had decided to possess us.

Unlike Sevasti, however, we do not pay Yanni for his services. If we offered him money he would throw it at us. Yet what would we do without him? It is he who mends the ever-collapsing doors and windows, he who wrestles with the recalcitrant toilet and the stubborn drain-pipes, he who makes little refinements for my kitchen — breadboards and rolling pins and a wonderful coolsafe which George sketched from the memory of the Coolgardie safes of his Australian childhood (a simple but miraculous device of hessian walls on a wood frame, with a tin tray of water on top that seeps down through dangling bits of flannel to wet the hessian and keep all our food cool and fresh and free of ants and flies).

It was Yanni too who arranged for the children to start school, thus relieving me of those three morning hours of supervising their lessons and forcing them to learn Greek. It was Yanni who consoled them when their pet rabbit died and Yanni who climbed the mountains before dawn to find them a new one and made a little house with a hinged door and a rainproof roof for it to live in.

He is the leader of most of our expeditions. He knows instinctively what we are looking for and he has an astonishing knack of rustling up old stories and songs and ancient women weaving rugs and wedding feasts and bottles of the rare, brusque wine of Kalymnos that is so difficult to find. He knows where the mysterious Cave of the Seven Maidens is and, unlike most of the Kalymnians, who believe it to be a place of malevolence, he is not afraid to penetrate its gloomy depths. It was Yanni who first told us the story of the Dorians coming to Kalymnos and who discovered at Argos an ancient stone with a sphinx carved on it. He knows which houses have the finest *ikons* and where you can get ancient *amphoras* dredged up from beneath the sea. He knows the names of all the herbs that grow and what uses can be made of them. He is highly intelligent, imaginative, sensitive and occasionally, even poetic. The glances of his soft eyes are tempered always with enquiry, as if he is looking out from his private world and wondering what on earth goes on in ours. But his tongue is the rough slurred dialect of the island, his grammar negligible, his vocabulary limited. When we sit drinking *retzina* around the black-and-white-checked cloth in Skeftarios' *taverna* while Emmanuele Manglis, the old diver, tells stories of sponges and sharks and cities under the sea in his pure and melodious Greek — for Manglis was once a university man and speaks the scholar's 'old' Greek — poor Yanni cannot understand a word.

He is pathetically defensive about his lack of education and quick to rise to Sevasti's caustic little baits. She knows all his little prides and vanities and how to prick him till he smarts. This, combined with his naive jealousy of his position in our house as friend and confidant, obliges one to tread cautiously.

I am tempted to point out that Sevasti is also our friend and to ask what the devil does it matter whether he or I or Sevasti or George or the children knock at the farmhouse door and ask for a pitcher of water. I hold my tongue.

For here we are confronted with something far more serious and meaningful than the mere pricking of Yanni's sense of dignity. Fetching water is a woman's work. Indeed, anything that involves the carrying of a burden is woman's work, whether it is stumbling down the mountain under a hundredweight of gorse for the bread ovens or carrying the roped sea chest to the departing sponge boat.

Kalymnian men, like old Etonians, do not carry parcels. They swing key chains. They play with tasselled strings of beads or shells. Sometimes they twirl a carnation between their fingers or carry it, gipsy-fashion, in their strong white teeth. Anything more burdensome is carried by their wives or sisters or mothers or daughters, who plod several paces behind, if not on the opposite side of the road.

In a crowded bus or an inter-island caique packed like a slave ship it is the woman who rises to give her seat to the man. I shall never forget the expression of horror on George's face one day in a crowded bus when an old woman who must have been seventy, and was infirm at that, was furiously berated by the driver for not instantly offering her seat. Because of her arthritic condition it had taken her a few seconds to lever herself up. Her own expression, when George insisted on her remaining seated and even relieved her of her heavier bundles, was one of acute embarrassment.

Kalymnos is probably one of the few surviving islands where one can see the worn threads of the old pattern, older than mainland Greece, in its essentials older than recorded history, going back to a misty time when masculine subjugation to an all-powerful Earth Mother led to masculine revolt and the goddess was overthrown. Then, because the men were still afraid, it was necessary to enslave the goddess, to deride her, to bolster up the new disquiet of freedom by boasts and jeers and laughter.

These dark atavistic currents still seem to swirl through the everyday life of Kalymnos. I suspect that it is because of them that Yanni finds such a source of embarrassment in our more emancipated domestic arrangements. If he comes upon George washing dishes or bathing the children he laughs uneasily and makes forced little jokes, but his eyes are carefully turned away, as though it would be impolite to look directly at my husband's degradation.

I am increasingly aware of the danger that this attitude may be contagious. George, who in the ten years of our married life has ungrudgingly washed dishes, made beds, changed babies' diapers, set the tea-table or gone shopping if I happened to be writing a piece and he was free, now becomes slightly defensive himself and makes curious little jests about aprons and who wears the pants that seem to me to be only slightly less uneasy than those of Yanni. He makes unnecessarily elaborate explanations of our working system, which has always seemed to me to be a perfectly reasonable one. We are both writers. Indeed, three of our novels, including the one we were working on at the time, were written in collaboration. Obviously an all-embracing co-operation, when necessary, is the only workable arrangement. But I have a faint gnawing suspicion that there will come a time when I will somehow find myself several paces in the rear, watching the flick of his key chain and quite unable to catch up because of the weight of the baggage I am carrying.

There is a young woman here who, although of Greek parentage, was born and raised in the United States. A few years ago she married a fairly wealthy young Kalymnian sponge merchant who had been educated in England and had spent most of his life abroad.

They were, she told me perplexedly, very happy indeed when they first came to Kalymnos. Their attitudes were mutually

44

emancipated and flavoured with Western sophistication. They had considered the Kalymnian customs just 'too quaint for words' and used to laugh together about them. The change came about so gradually that even now she cannot quite put her finger on the first warning sign. It might have been the Sunday evening in Agios Christos when, instead of standing by her side as usual, her husband had stepped forward briskly and with never a backward glance and she had found herself wedged inextricably among the pious Kalymnian wives, watching her husband on the opposite side of the nave triumphantly chanting his *Kyrié Eleisons* amid a solid wall of men. Or perhaps the first really disturbing change was on that evening when he (who had been so devoted and attentive) summoned her all the way in from the kitchen to where he sat browsing through a week-old Athens newspaper and ordered her to fetch him a clean pocket handkerchief.

'And would you believe it, honey,' she confessed sadly, 'I was so taken aback I fetched it for him! I was done for from that moment on. It's got so bad now that the other day — I'm not kidding — the other day he asked me why I didn't stand up when he came into the room! I'm only telling you,' she added soberly, 'so you'll be warned. Keep a sharp watch, dear, and pounce right down at that first sign!'

On the surface of it Kalymnos is absolutely a man's world. Girls and boys are to some extent segregated from the time they are quite small. Even though Kalymnians are the most aquatic of all islanders, little boys and girls of five and six and seven have separate areas of play in the sea. The boundaries are fluid, and they cross and recross and jumble together while they are still small, but as they grow older this segregation becomes distinct and rigid. Nubile girls and women not only swim in concealed coves and beaches away from the eyes of men but wear (except for the rich or educated who have learned foreign customs) an enveloping garment that is rather like a square-necked nightgown. Actually it is very graceful and pretty. It is usually made of plain bright cotton banded about neck and sleeves with another colour, so a group of women going into the sea achieve a formal, fluid grace of line and colour that you will never find on Western beaches. But if the purpose of the garment is modesty it defeats itself, for the moment it is wet it becomes transparent and clings provocatively to breast and belly and thighs.

('*You* admire them going into the water, my sweet,' says George, blissfully stuffing himself with black figs under the twisted tree where we have paused to rest above the little pebbled cove. 'Just tell me when they are coming out.')

Obviously, too, in this trammelling garment the women's aquatic exercises are restricted. They never manage anything more strenuous than the breaststroke, the sidestroke or a form of gentle dog paddle. One day I was lured by an overweening pride into demonstrating the Australian crawl. The women, after their first stunned and gratifying surprise, averted their eyes. My performance, I realised, was to them something as grotesque as a trapeze act or a performing seal.

'Only men swim like that,' Yanni's wife Polymnea whispered to me in embarrassed explanation. After a moment of troubled thought she added, 'If you like I'll make you a *fustani* to swim in. Your skin is going quite black.'

Once or twice Yanni, greatly daring and trying hard to look as if it were the most natural thing in the world, swam alone with George and me. I think Polymnea was never told of these excursions, which resulted in intense humiliation for Yanni, who found to his horror and bewilderment that I could swim faster than he. The indignity of being beaten by a woman was more than he could bear, and he went back to swimming some distance away from us, I suspect so that he could practice the crawl stroke, an innovation in Kalymnian swimming, unobserved.

One day we were shown over the orphanage by the *despotis*, or bishop, a gentle, strong man from Istanbul whose diocese is the three islands of Kalymnos, Leros and Astypalaia. He founded the orphanage some years ago and maintains it now with a fatherly solicitude and care that is warm and happy. There is nothing institutional in the character of the place. All the children in the big white house are girls, whose ages range from a baby of a few months to eighteen years. They were all particularly happy on the day of our visit because one of the older girls had just been married to the little round smiling personal assistant to the *despotis*. (A Greek priest can be married before final ordination, although if he does marry he can never rise higher than ordinary parish priest.) The bishop regards all the girls as his own daughters and arranges their marriages most carefully.

We were both very much impressed by the genuine affection existing between the splendid bearded patriarchal figure in his blue silk and black taffeta hung with great crosses of silver and coloured enamel and the little girls yelping in from school to kiss him and hug him and proudly show him the marks in their exercise books. He even took a hand at giving the baby its bottle, but without great skill. He seemed genuinely upset at his failure.

Was there, George asked, a similar institution for boys?

'Oh no. Boys are not in the same moral danger.'

Moral danger. One hears it again and again. A girl is exposed to moral danger if she wears lipstick, cuts her hair, sits in a street cafe (although it is permitted in summer, when the tables are moved across the street to the edge of the sea — she may then take ice-cream or lemonade), drinks anything stronger than the sickly-sweet *gazoza*, voices an opinion on anything deeper than culinary matters or herbal lore or dances with a partner face to face instead of side by side. (Again I except the rich and the educated, who have exchanged the wonderful native dances for the tango and the mambo, which they dance self-consciously at one another's houses and, in summer, incongruously, on the threshing floor at Brosta.) I do not include in this list being alone with a man. If by some miraculous conjunction of circumstances a Kalymnian girl did manage to be alone with a man even for only a few minutes she would no longer be merely exposed to moral danger. She would be finished. Not only would that man not marry her — unless forced to do so, as he could be, by the police — but no other man would either. Even if the limit of her depravity had been the singing of a two-part song of holding hands or watching the moon rise over the mountains of Kos, the unwritten law would be inflexible.

47

Very occasionally, for the most rigid of codes can never entirely crush human nature, one hears of an illicit affair. It is spoken of as something of phenomenal and historic significance, like the Saint George's Day earthquake that destroyed Kos, and the end of the story invariably relates the brutal and bloody beating of the girl by brothers or father, never of vengeance wreaked on the seducer.

There was one young girl a few years ago who somehow managed to conduct her love affair in secret to the stage of pregnancy. The young man naturally refused to marry her. Kalymnian men don't marry damaged goods, even if they have done the damaging. The poor girl somehow managed to keep her state secret ('She was fat, anyway,' says Yanni. 'No one would notice much when she got a bit fatter.') and gave birth to her baby alone in a shed at the back of the house. She wrapped the child in newspapers and buried it under some stones on the slope of the mountains, where it was discovered some weeks later by a shepherd boy. Unfortunately the family name was written on the newspaper, and the girl was discovered. She and her faithless lover were taken to Rhodes by the police. There, apparently, the violence of her hatred and revulsion for the man commanded the respect even of the Church. It didn't avail her much, though, for she came back married to the man and has borne him three more children since. People say that they get along very well, all things considered. After all, they point out, she was lucky that her father didn't kill her.

It is impossible not to be aware of the deep and profound difference between male and female here. A boy of twelve is still a child, irresponsible, extroverted, impulsive in thought and action. A girl of the same age is already a woman, secret, reserved, circumspect, dignified, responsible. And strong.

I think that here women are never quite regarded as human beings. They are of a different species — the female species, the mysterious Other Ones whose femaleness is derided and despised, but who must be kept under lock and key in case they work a magic. It is all very dark and ancient and filled with the cold white beams of the moon, the fear of blood and three spits for the evil eye. In the churches the dark, hard God of Byzantium thunders His creed of male supremacy. In the *tavernas* and coffee-houses and shipyards and the crowded diving boats speeding to the shores of Africa it is substantiated. But in the Kalymnian houses the triple goddess lurks still upon the hearth and bedshelf, smiling lewdly among the *ikons*.

For the apparent fact of male supremacy must be set against the older and more significant fact that property here descends through the female line, from mother to eldest daughter.

A girl must bring to marriage a house, the requisite furnishings, bed linen and kitchen equipment and usually a sum of money as well. This is called *prika*, and rich and many are the jests among the young men concerning the amount of *prika* they judge their virility to be worth. They need bring to the marriage nothing more than this virility. Parents accordingly dread the birth of girl children as we might dread the birth of a child deformed or spastic. The affection lavished on daughters later is in inverse proportion to the miserable reception given to them on their entry into the world, for every girl means another house to be bought and furnished. And for all their masculine supremacy fathers must go to the ends of the earth and the bottom of the sea to earn the money for these dowries. And mothers begin making lace for the marriage sheets the moment they are up from the lying-in couch.

Marriages are arranged early — by the parents. The young men or girls have little or nothing to say in the matter, and there is no courting. Either the boy's parents or the girl's can make the first approach, and after that it becomes a matter for family councils. To these councils the young man, but not the girl, is admitted. The potential bridegroom and all his family advisers sit around a feast table, and the *prika* is discussed over platters of *smarithes* and *palamethes* and *dolmadhes* and dogfish in garlic sauce and the circling decanters of *retzina*. If the family has already decided on the girl the young man has no hope, even if his prospective wife has a harelip, a forty-inch waist or the tongue of a shrew. They will bully and badger and cajole and threaten him around the table all through the night and all next day if necessary. It is certain that he will not rise from this feast of the third degree until he has surrendered his acquiescence.

In the meantime the girl waits with her mother in her own house — whether it be for three hours or thirty — to know whether or not she is acceptable. If the young man's family has decided finally in her favour and the victim's exhausted agreement been obtained a deputation calls at her house and invites her father and brothers to join in the feast and discussion. Again the prospective bride is not invited. Hers is a role of mute patience. She makes her first appearance at the engagement party, which, because everything now moves at an urgent tempo, is held as soon as possible, sometimes even the day after the family council. The girl's mother gives her a plain gold ring, and the boy's father gives him one exactly the same. These rings will be exchanged on the wedding day, which usually is on the first Sunday after the engagement.

The bride's friends arrive early to bathe her and dress her and sing the wedding songs, and all the old women who can pack into the room sit around with gnarled hands folded across their high stomachs, watching the girl with bright, lewd, curious eyes.

The chosen couple walk to church together followed by as many men, women and children as can crowd inside. With chanting and candles and wreaths of white wax flowers the two young strangers are bound together and bidden to be fertile. Rice is thrown at them as they circle three times around the great silver Bible, and the chandeliers are set swinging in glittering arcs above their heads. As the church bells begin to clang the bridal couple is led away by singing priests. All the people follow, and the procession winds chanting up the rubbled mountain streets to one of the tiny coloured cubes on the hill.

Even if the house has only one room (and not many have more) hundreds of people will come for the party. Chairs will be borrowed from all the neighbours and placed around the bare floor, circle within circle, until there is only a dancing space a few feet wide in the centre. There will be a violin, a couple of round-bellied *bouzoukia*, perhaps a zither, sometimes a *tsabuna*, a primitive mountain bagpipe made from the whole skin of a sheep, with horn and pipe of carved olive root. There will be plates of sticky cake dripping with honey, little thimble glasses of *strega* and Samian cherry brandy.

As the afternoon wears on the *retzina* jars appear, fifty kilos at a time in enormous wicker-covered flasks, and dishes of fish and meatballs, octopus and potatoes — food strong enough to sustain the guests over a whole night's dancing and drinking. For the dancing will go on until dawn, sometimes all through the following day. And while one guest remains, even though he be too drunk to move, the bridal pair must sit and smile, maintaining a pretence of enjoying the jests that grow earthier as the *retzina* jars are emptied and morning draws near.

By the time the last dancer has gone the bridal couple are white and exhausted, looking more than ever like garlanded sacrifices. But they must still endure the last family gathering in the room that now looks as if an earthquake has struck it. They must make a token meal, respond to the toasts, heed quietly the advice that is given them separately by their parents. It is all rather like two fighters in a prize ring being given instructions by their seconds before the last round begins. The Kalymnian custom generally follows that the bridal couple are then locked in the house and the key taken away by the bride's mother, who will not unlock the door again for three days.

Yanni, whose marriage was arranged while he was away soldiering in Italy, had never even seen Polymnea before his betrothal. The marriage took place on the following Sunday. He told us, 'I will never forget that third morning. I tried the doorhandle and it *opened!* I crossed myself and thanked God for his goodness and ran out into the street and all the way to Lavassi. I scrambled over rocks and stones and chased the goats and stood singing on the mountain for an hour or more. And after that I scrambled down again and flung off all my clothes and swam so far out to sea I thought I'd never be able to swim back. I drank *retzina*, and I did the rounds of the *tavernas* and coffeehouses with my friends, and I knew that I had never appreciated them before. I didn't get home until two in the morning!'

'Did Polymnea flee to her friends too?' I asked.

'Ah no,' said Yanni. 'Polymnea was sleeping. Polymnea,' he added with a little pride, 'slept for a week.'

When the door is unlocked the first visitors are the mothers of the bride and the bridegroom, come solely for the purpose of examining the sheets. If the evidence is satisfactory the bed linen is taken to the sea for ritual washing, a long process involving spells and incantations. But woe betide the bride whose marriage bed is unstained. The bridegroom's mother can go straight to the *despotis* and demand that the marriage be annulled.

I thought this was pretty awful and one-sided until it occurred to me that even in such a case it is not the woman who is turned out of the house. It is the man. The house belongs to the woman, and so does everything in it. The ignominy of leaving the newly fitted, cosy home is borne by the man, and I wonder in how many cases young bridegrooms have overruled their outraged mothers on this technicality of the marriage sheets.

From the time of her marriage (usually when she is aged from fifteen to seventeen) the primary function of a Kalymnian woman is reproduction, at which, heaven knows, she acquits herself honourably. She will have a baby every year for as long as she is capable. And since midwifery is on a plane of medieval crudity it is seldom more than a couple of years before her breasts begin to sag, her teeth to fall out, her waist and buttocks to broaden and begin to jelly as she walks. Whatever character she might possess is in this fecund phase submerged beneath her overwhelming, enslaving femaleness. And she *is* enslaved — enslaved to the species. A Kalymnian woman of thirty is utterly sexual. She is a large, soft, white, secretive, slow-moving thing. ('If you cut a slit in one,' says George in mild fascination, 'you would find her *full of eggs*!') In her youth she is a graceful *kore* from a vase painting, but in her maturity she is Rhea, Mother of the Universe, hatching out the great stone.

But after the menopause and the end of her child-bearing — by which time she will have produced anything from six to sixteen children, the majority of whom, surprisingly, have survived — she emerges again, high-stomached and sibylline, freed of the burden of her body, with hooded eyes and the carved, still face of

Hecate. Often the metamorphosis produces a particular beauty, more of character perhaps than feature, but compelling none the less. In her full black skirts and tightly wound coif she is a mysterious and terrible being now, particularly when her body is bent by the repetitive years of conception, gestation and suckling, and she walks with a curved stick, like a Hoffman witch. Now is her hour. Desire no longer plagues her. She is deaf to the clamour of the unborn. She is the wise and fearsome old woman of legend and, having bought her wisdom in a hard market, she guards it jealously. Hers is the secret of the evil eye, the key in the cake, the lore of graveyard and coffin, the spells and charms and love potions. It is she who ushers you into the world, and she who closes your eyes when you leave it. She knows the meaning of your dreams, reads a future from the grains in your coffee cup. And it is she who materialises on every Kalymnian mountain, her apron filled with strange herbs and grasses, and an old cracked song on her lips.

'*Gorgonas!*' says Yanni and shudderingly sketches his cross.

'*Gorgonaiki!*' Mikailis says angrily to his baby daughter, who is crying in the hammock again.

'Hurry up there, little *gorgonas*,' Petros snaps at the three little girls sent to fetch his flagon of Lipsian wine.

Now the *gorgonas*, as everyone well knows, were three frightful maidens of legend, Stheno, Euryale and Medusa. They had wings, claws, enormous teeth and lethal eyes. Medusa, the one mortal sister of the three and mother, by the ubiquitous Poseidon, of Chrysaor and Pegasus, was eventually slain by Perseus, and her frightful head was placed by Athena in the centre of her shield. In a rather refined form it survives still on the back of the Greek twenty-*drachmae* banknote. From the other two sisters, Yanni contends, descend the women of Kalymnos.

'Don't you be misled,' he warns darkly. 'The men don't rule here. The *gorgonas* do. Our only use is to make children and go out to work for them.'

The constant bitter reference to women as *gorgonas* is very interesting, particularly, as Mr Robert Graves points out, as

Medusa was once the triple-goddess herself, hiding behind a prophylactic Gorgon mask and Perseus in the story represented the patriarchal Hellenes who invaded Greece and Asia Minor in the second millennium B.C., overran the goddess's chief shrines, stripped her priestesses of their Gorgon masks and overthrew her.

Certainly Kalymnian domestic relationships seem curious to us. Wives and husbands appear to share little of each other's lives except meals and the bedshelf. The bonds that hold them together are secret and complex, full of the strength of indifference, with this unceasing antagonism of sex against sex to exasperate every issue, and, in its own queer way, to cement the union.

When husbands emigrate, as they are doing at the rate of hundreds a year, the wives seldom accompany them. Often they do not even want to follow later. There are many women here whose husbands have been away for years. They seem perfectly content with this arrangement.

'When do you intend to follow your husband?' I asked one of them one day.

She looked at me in some surprise. 'Oh, *I'm* not leaving Kalymnos,' she said. 'My house is here, and my children. We have good fig trees and grapes and sweet water in the well. My husband sends me good money every month and parcels of clothes. Why should I want to leave?'

I thought of her husband working on a hydro-electric project in Tasmania, ten thousand miles away. 'But don't you want to be together?' I asked boldly. She did not appear to understand. She had a good house here, she repeated, and sweet water in the well.

'But the children?' I said. 'Surely you would like the children to have a better chance in life than it's possible for them to find here?'

'Ah, the children ...' she considers the matter half-heartedly. The children might join their father later, when they were grown a little. The boys, anyway. All boys had to go away, yes. But the girls would have their houses here, as she had, because her husband was sending back good money. All the girls would have *prika*. Why should they want to leave?

I studied the children curiously. She had eight — thin, wiry little boys with shaven heads and limbs like sticks, plumper, stronger-looking girls who were beginning to toss their long, matted hair and to glance sideways from eyes like big dark pools. One girl was sweetly bosomed already, and it was clear that the subject of *prika* was soon to be transferred from an economic to a physical plane. She stood behind her elder brother's chair, serving him with stewed beans from the big cooking pot. He sprawled like a young lord with his legs stretched beneath the table, watching the women scurry to serve him.

But it will be he who will go to the ends of the earth and face dangers and disasters and humiliations he does not dream of yet so that his sisters can sit among the growing vines and fig trees on a fine spring morning and count up their *prika*. He may not even marry until every one of them is wed, no matter how he loves. Kalymnos is a barren rock, but the women have sent their roots down deep into it, and there is nothing for the men but the far lands or the sea.

5

I sit with Irini on the whitewashed step of her little blue house on the mountainside. Below us the rooftops have picked up a random crop of spring grass. They descend in oblongs of viridian to the harbour below, where two hundred coloured boats ride gently on a sea that is viridian too, and shining in the sun.

The town is spread out beneath us like a patchwork quilt thrown carelessly down in the valley between the mountains. Here we are five hundred feet above the harbour and the shopping streets, but the encircling ring of mountains gives the illusion of having gained in height and pressed in closer. The rock wall, scarred and fissured, seems gaunter and more menacing from here than when seen from the town below, perhaps because here one is part of it.

The view is stupendous. In Kalymnos panorama is the prerogative of the poor. On the mountainside water is not easy to come by. There are no roads or streets, only goat trails scribbled through the ochreous clay, scoured watercourses choked with boulders and pebbles and occasionally a crude elevation of steps made of rocks piled one on top of the other. On these slopes a pair of shoes will not last ten days. There is a reason other than poverty why everyone goes barefoot. Moreover, the town's skimpy electricity supply, which elsewhere functions spasmodically between sundown and midnight, does not reach this far. Here you will see life illuminated as it was three thousand years ago — by a wick of homespun wool floating in a shallow bowl of oil. This is an area that has no name. The people refer to it merely as *epano* — above.

But a rich man would pay handsomely for the view thrown in for the three shillings a week Irini pays in rent. A rich man, that is to say, from some other country. The rich of Kalymnos cling to the flat securities five hundred feet below, where water flows, roads are paved, lights usually flick on at the touch of a switch, and the shops are handy. There they huddle within their sheltering walls and gardens, close to the amenities, close to the comfort of the radio programmes from Athens, close to one another. Their walls and trees block out the mountains and the sea. Irini rises to the dawn coming golden out of Turkey.

To the left the valley curls away towards Chorio and Brosta, flanked on either side by cliffs and crumbling citadels and gouged-out caves to remind one of the time, nine hundred years ago, when pirates ruled the island. Behind these eroded mementoes of bloodier days the mountains rise in bleak, beautiful outlines. As they recede their harsh shapes become more weird, their summits higher, so that the perspective — and in Greece perspective is always a tricky thing — gives the queer impression that the mountains are moving towards you, their peaks hanging over as if they are about to topple like a breaking wave.

The view seaward is, if possible, even more magnificent. Below, at the edge of the harbour, people the size of ants are moving about their business on the Plateia Kharalampos, but not too fast, for it is February and the sun is warm. We can see Mikailis, Irini's husband, dragging a *carro* along the thin pier where the stout-bellied schooner from Amorgos is berthed, unloading timber. (In Kalymnos men are the beasts of burden. There are no cranes for unloading the ships, no horses to drag the carts, no trucks to move the cargo. The heavy handcarts, cruelly laden, are pulled along by the men, men like Mikailis, sweating on the thick dragropes, rubbing calluses into their shoulders, twisting their bodies out of shape. If Mikailis works solidly through a ten-hour day he may earn about twenty-five shillings. His earnings in a good week, for there are few days that will provide ten hours of work, may amount to a little more than £3 10s. More usually it is about thirty-five shillings, upon which he supports a wife and six children!)

Beyond the crowded harbour stretches the long rocky snout of Cali Point. The sea is that unbelievable blue which seems to exist only in the Aegean. The satellite islands of Kalymnos, Plateia and Pserimos sit into the sea — Plateia, with its flat surface and the milled edges of its yellow cliffs, has the appearance of a golden sovereign; the humpy central hill of Pserimos and its darker colouring give it a striking resemblance to a bossed shield lying flat on the water — but across the gulf the island of Kos has miraculously lifted itself out of the water. It runs almost the length of the horizon, stretched out along a broad band of luminous air that divides sea from sky. Oromédhon, its lovely central mountain, is capped with little white clouds like puffballs. To the left of Kos a caique sails in the narrow strait. Behind it, dream-pale in the shining air, are the Turkish islands, the headland of Halicarnassus and the pink pinnacles of the Anatolian mountains. Behind Kos to the right rise the three lumpy crags of distant Nissiros. On the northern slopes of Kos the sun glitters white on the houses of Pyli. In the gulf there are nine fishing boats with red sails.

Irini is sorting good beans from bad in a big tin tray held in her lap. Around her bare big toe is hooked the string of a tiny hammock made from a scrap of striped blanket and a few lengths of seamen's rope. In this the baby Anna swings backward and forward above the huge built-in bedshelf that takes up half the space of the house.

The communal bedshelf is the most striking and, aesthetically at least, the most attractive feature of Kalymnian houses. As most Kalymnian houses consist, like Irini's, of only a single room, whole families must obviously sleep together, with small babies slung in improvised hammocks overhead. I have seen one family of ten sleeping like peas in a pod along the railed-in, unmattressed shelf, with four hammocks swinging above. The children on the shelf below awaken every now and then to give a tug on the ropes attached to the babies slung above them, like a team of dazed bellringers! When childhood gives way to maturity the bedshelf must, I suppose, in the case of mixed families have its element of embarrassment, although certain nuances of immodesty are avoided by the fact that all Kalymnian families, at least in the poorer houses, seem to go to bed with their clothes on. I remember one night calling unexpectedly on a family in Lavassi, and surprising them all in bed together, the father and mother, three grown-up daughters who had had sophisticated educations in Athens, and two husky sons considerably past the age of puberty. They all sat up like cut-out figures in a shooting gallery, pulling the blankets around their shoulders and blinking self-consciously.

Around us on the rubbled mountainside, among the pecking hens and scraggy goats and a confusion of pigs, ducks, skinny cats and mongrel dogs, Irini's other five children are playing with a horde of neighbours and cousins. My two are distinguishable only by their fair hair. After three months they are beginning to look as bruised and scarred and scruffy as their playmates, although in their play they are still inclined to be either lordly or apprehensive.

'Ah well, God sends them,' Irini says, vaguely surveying the swarms of children tumbling among the stones. She has a very beautiful face and an entire set of stainless-steel teeth. When she opens her mouth she glitters brilliantly, and one has an uneasy sense of the miraculous, as if the silver *ikon* above the bedshelf had made a pronouncement.

At the thought of children she begins automatically to unbutton the front of her bodice. The second youngest, Georgios, who is already walking, scrabbles into her lap and upsets the tray of beans, which rattle and scatter all over the steps, bringing all the hens striding in a cackle of excitement. For a moment Irini studies the dented tray, the broadcast dinner, the wildly pecking hens as if she might cry.

But Georgios has pulled her breast from her bodice and is holding it in both filthy little hands while he sucks away greedily.

Her face, her whole body, relaxes. Her mouth curves over an arc of silver. She cuffs him affectionately.

'Eeeh! Not *you*! There will be nothing left for the baby!' But she does not pull him away. There will be plenty left for the baby, and all the babies to come. She is still only twenty-five, and it is almost certain that she will double her present family before she has finished. 'Calliope!' she calls. 'Themolena! Petros! Come and pick up these beans if you want to eat today!'

Going down the mountain I turn and look back at her. She is still sitting on the step in the open doorway, with the small bullet head of Georgios nuzzling at her breast and her bare foot moving rhythmically on the hammock string. The children are down on all fours among the boulders, scrabbling for beans, and the incensed hens are pouncing and pecking in a whirr of angry wings. A brown goat sniffs acquisitively at the washing strung from the window. The sun glints on Irini's miraculous *ikonic* smile as she raises her arm in farewell.

I turn and reach for the hands of my two children. It is an involuntary action, defensive, a sudden need for reassurance. But Martin and Shane, impatient of restraining hands, are gone already, pelting down the mountainside. I can see them hurtling one behind the other down the narrow descending alleyways — Martin's leaping legs are like long blue scissors snapping; Shane's yellow hair streams behind her. What tall children they are, I realise suddenly; how independent they have become!

I climb slowly down to the shining sea, haunted by a vague, hollow sense of loneliness and loss.

George, rather abstracted and with a smudge of ink from the typewriter ribbon on his nose, lets us in. For a moment he looks at me curiously.

'Why, what's happened?' he says. 'You've been crying.'

6

When the first Ptolemy established the great library of Alexandria some three hundred years before the Christian era one of the books included was a manual of the ancient astrologers. In this were listed 'all those poor and miserable wretches whom we hold to have been born under some disastrous conjunction of planetary influences, and whose lot in life places them at a level of existence no better, and often worse, than the beasts of the field.' Prominent in this list were *the divers for sponges, who die early in their youth, since theirs is a dangerous trade.*

Yet how our hearts leap still at bravery. Martin's heart flies to his eyes whenever a sponge diver speaks to him, and George and I are no more blasé. We have never known men like these before.

There are about fifteen hundred divers in the town, and to understand the problem and poverty of Kalymnos it is essential first to grasp the fact that the island's total population of fourteen thousand lives on the courage and endurance of these few.

Apart from an inconsiderable export trade in oranges from the little port of Vathy, there is no other worthwhile industry on the island. The bare rock is cut by two parallel valleys three miles apart. The first curls across between the mountains from Pothia, the port and principal town, to the summer houses at Brosta, on the north coast looking across to the spectacular island of Telendos. The other, slightly more fertile valley also runs clear across the island, from the picturesque cliff-walled port of Vathy to Merthies, the next summer settlement to Brosta. In these two valleys grow citrus fruits, olives, figs, grapes, certain vegetables and a few meagre crops of grain. Everywhere there is a great deal of prickly pear, which is widely relished as a summer delicacy. Apart from these two valleys and a few acres of scant pasture around the convents and monasteries in the hills there is no other cultivable land on Kalymnos. The rest is rock. The true pastures of Kalymnos are in the surrounding sea.

The sponge boats leave in April or early May. Between sixty and a hundred of them sail out to Alexandria and Derna and Crete and Benghazi and Tripoli. For a few weeks before their departure, when the banks advance the yearly loans to the captains, the town has a misleading air of prosperity. The boats must be equipped and stocked with food for seven months. Money is in circulation — millions, even billions of *drachmae!* Children appear in cheap new dresses, new sandals. This is the time for weddings, for christenings, for parties. In the *tavernas* and coffee-houses business booms. The gambling tables have the air and atmosphere of a little Monte Carlo. Men walk the streets with a springier step, as if it were really their money and not the banks'.

All summer long, while the boats are away, the town lies in a torpor of heat and idleness. Everyone who can goes to the other side of the island, to little houses at Brosta or Merthies. If one has no house he erects a makeshift tent of striped rugs strung on bamboo poles. For the hot months Kalymnians live close to the sea on the fish they catch and the figs and prickly pear and grapes that grow around them and the sweet water from the wells. There is a charming unwritten law that any person, man, woman or child, may satisfy his hunger by taking what fruit he can eat from anybody's property, so long as he eats it there by the tree or the vine. He is only guilty of theft if he carries the fruit away in a basket or stuffed into his pocket to eat later.

During these months buying and selling are practically at a standstill. There will be no money coming in until the boats return late in autumn. There are no tourists to bring in a little summer revenue. Summer buying, pared down to barest essentials, is almost all done on credit.

This somnolent summer of the island's stay-at-homes is in startling contrast to the brutal slavery in the boats working the sponge-beds off Africa. These boats are built to a standard pattern in the Lavassi shipyards in the next cove around from the town — twenty-nine feet long, of Samian pine and totally devoid of any special comforts, working boats. In each of them any number from twelve to twenty men will live cooped up together for six or seven months, and most of them will not set foot on land again until they return to Kalymnos.

Theirs is an existence very close to the lowest common denominator of living. Their daily lot is danger, hardship, privation. They live at sea on one meal a day, because it is dangerous to dive with food in the stomach. The skin divers, who work naked, without suits or masks, plunge to the bottom of the sea as many as fifty times a day, often to depths of one hundred and fifty feet and even more. The masked *ferneze* divers and the helmeted *skafendros*, who work on air lines, make only three dives a day, but they stay down for periods from half an hour to an hour and a half at a time, depending on the depth of water.

The work of these divers is harsh and terrible. The season is short and the harvest unpredictable, and they must take enough sponges to repay the money advanced to the captains, and through the captains to their wives and families, and to cover the diving licence, which is now about £1,000 to dive off the African coast, before there is any profit in the sponges.

In the good years, the nostalgic, sighed-for years that are gone, a good diver in a good season was able to make as much as £700 a year. Today about the best he can expect is £300. Usually it is much less than that. And this is all he will earn in the whole year.

The men come back in late October or November, physically ill from malnutrition, exposure and exhaustion, with their harvest of sponges, their dozen or so newly made cripples, and a few bundles of clothes and personal possessions to give to the families of the six or seven dead buried somewhere on the sandy shores of Africa.

In some degree or other all the population of Kalymnos lives parasitically upon these unfortunate few.

'The crazy men!' Georgios calls them. Georgios is a wealthy and cynical sponge dealer. Although Kalymnian by birth, he has his home and his warehouse in Piraeus. We met him first in the little blue and pink *taverna* run by Corfu Costas next to the smelly and ramshackle barn which is the only movie theatre on the island and is happily dignified by the name *Cinema Splendide*. He speaks, among his seven languages, fluent English and has an illogical passion for the waltzes of Franz Léhar.

He was, he told us sadly, returning to Piraeus on the following day, his buying having been completed and there being no other compelling reason why he should stay on in the place he loved so dearly.

This first meeting was in the middle of January. At the end of July Georgios was still postponing his return to Piraeus and drinking his way around the Kalymnian *tavernas*. His wife, he told us, glancing with melancholy envy at the poster of the strong man tacked to the wall above the blue *retzina* barrels, had taken legal action to forbid him re-entry into the house, having assumed his long absence to mean that he had abandoned her. He told us he intended contesting the matter, but, alas, we never did hear how the story ended.

Georgios, during the protracted enjoyment of his absenteeism, spent every night in the *tavernas*, drinking with the divers. His fellow merchants, more snobbish, limit their social intercourse to contacts with their own kind in the big white houses that lie well away from the sea. They were inclined to censure Georgios for choosing his company in the waterside *tavernas*.

'Look,' said Georgios, 'every *drachma* I own is by virtue of the fact that one of these crazy men has risked his life to get it for me. The least I can do is to buy him a drink!'

'Big fish eat little fish,' he would say sourly, speaking of the economics of the sponge business. 'What do you think of our Kalymnian bread? Strong, isn't it? It has blood and salt in it as well as flour.'

But Georgios is a rare merchant. His sensitivity is delicate. Besides being hounded by a sense of guilt that he feels he must pay in beakers of *retzina* he is drawn to the divers, as we are, by the vicarious sense of danger and excitement a restricted physical existence borrows from reckless, expansive lives. Sponges mean nothing to him — they are a commodity he trades in. But he knows what they mean to the men who get them. It is perhaps because of this that he is the only merchant the divers will easily tolerate.

The summer's harvest is piled in soft salty mountains in every sponge room and warehouse in the town. There seem to be an incredible number of sponges. The road in front of the huge Vouvalis warehouse is paved with them, like a strange yellow growth sprung through the cobbles overnight, and long lines of boys and men dance strangely all day in the wintry shallows of the sea, pounding bales of sponges underfoot. Surely there is not a single sponge left on the bottom of the ocean!

'But they aren't sponges, you see,' says Georgios. 'They are food for fourteen thousand people for a whole year. They are shoes for the children, *prika* for the daughters. They are work for the labourers and carpenters and tailors and plasterers and pastry cooks. They are new kitchen chairs and Sunday dresses. And names bought off the grocers' books. And God help us,' — he shakes his white mane of hair fiercely — 'there just aren't enough sponges to spread that far!'

On Kalymnos only the merchants live well. Some of them live very well indeed, almost in a state of feudal grandeur. They drink imported whisky and send their children to be educated abroad. But merchants have lived well since the first shrewd Neolithic fellow traded a chopping axe of chert for a hunting knife of obsidian, not because he wanted the knife, but because he knew his brother did. It is in the nature of merchants to live well.

The sponge boat captains, too, live in reasonable comfort — by Kalymnian standards, that is — and their daughters are usually well dowered. A few of the tradespeople of the town and the more important officials keep up a sort of genteel middle-class standard, usually reflected in the hideous veneer furniture with which they replace the infinitely lovelier native pieces inherited from their parents.

The divers live always on the raw edge of poverty.

This is deeply resented by the respectable citizens, not because of its basic unfairness, but because it represents an offence to their consciences. They are quick to find and apportion blame.

'I think it's disgusting!' says a tradesman's wife of my acquaintance. 'The way those men drink and gamble the money away as soon as they get home! They aren't off our books for more than a month in the year! If my husband didn't feel sorry for their poor, wretched women and children he wouldn't give a diver credit for anything in the world!'

I refrained from asking her what she thought would be left of her husband's business if he wiped the divers from his books.

It is perfectly true that the return of the boats is the signal for a wild and roistering season in Kalymnos. Gambling is intense. The *tavernas* are packed every night. It will continue through the winter for as long as the money lasts. Often it is gone by Christmas, and men are forced to go away again on dangerous winter cruises to earn enough to see them through until summer diving begins again. The crazy men. They gamble as though their lives depended on the throw of a dice, the turn of a card. They drink as if drunkenness were the only sanity. What other way is there for them to express their relief at having escaped whole from the seven months that lie behind them, or to ward off the approaching terror of the next season?

The crazy men, Georgios calls them. But in all the Kalymnian songs and poems they are the *pallikaria*, the heroes, the strong ones. All the amphibious play of the island's small boys, who swim like fish and fight like tigers, is keyed to this symbolism of the *pallikaria*. Its visual expression is a man with a strong, hard face, sunburned and weatherbeaten, a man with a black peaked sailor's cap and a high-necked jersey and haunted eyes.

For there is nothing heroic in the diver's attitude towards his work. There are no boastings, no bravadoes, no longshore self esteems. They hate their work. They speak of it gravely and with

66

a sort of subdued horror. They live all winter long in daily dread of that hour when they must wrap up their few belongings in a cheap checked tablecloth and be rowed off in the dinghy to the waiting boats to begin it all again.

'Ah, there's nothing grand or brave in it. It's ugly work, Charmian. Very ugly work.' This is Fotes speaking, a thin thirty-six-year-old diver with a flat, white, exhausted face and a swagger to his shoulders that suggests he is always on the verge of darting a fearful glance behind him. His tongue trips when he talks; his hands shake. He looks punchdrunk. He drinks rowdily every night, whipping up a wild, pathetic gaiety. He has the reputation of being a *kakos anthropos*, a bad man, easily inflamed to violence, although I personally have never known him to be other than courteous and gentle. They say that when he gets home at night he beats his wife. I should think it more likely that he goes to bed and cries.

Fotes is thirty-six years old and has been diving now for eighteen years. He has six children, but even if he were not so heavily burdened he would have no hope of ever emigrating because for a few months when he was younger he openly cast his lot with the Communists. They say he is a fine diver, if a reckless one.

There are no appointments in Samarra for Fotes and his kind. Samarra is where they were born. Their future does not sneak before them to wait in silent ambush. It lurches down the sunny street to meet them, trailing a twisted leg. It sits with them at the gambling tables, talking commonplaces. It is there behind the basket of peanuts their children clamour for. They drink their coffee facing a stick hooked over the next chair. They come from the *taverna* into the moonlit street to see the shadow stumbling on the wall.

Nowhere in Kalymnos can you escape it — the tapping stick, the uneven shuffle of the crippled men, the twisted silhouette against the sea. Like the sinister recurrent motif of an early Continental film it limps through the everydayness of eating and living and drinking and quarrelling and loving. It is the shadow the island casts.

There are divers who have worked every season for thirty years or more and have lived to run races with their grandchildren. But they are few. Old Stamatis talks in the *taverna* of that first summer, thirty-five years ago, and of the men who went away with him. By Jesus! he says, they were *divers* then! He rambles on with the story of the man who dived into the great shark's mouth and was vomited out again, and the story of the diver who was crippled and went to dive again the next season and was miraculously cured by the pressures that had twisted him the year before.

What happened to them all?

They are dead. All dead. Under the sea or the sand ...

7

The very old article beneath the hanging bunch of bay leaves has at last cracked up. George has reduced it to ruin in a demented attempt to rid its inner workings of a green apple dropped into it by Shane. All Mike's engineering skill can never make it function again.

Yanni says he knows a woman who is moving and will sell us hers. We decline the offer. The landlady cannot be found. Yanni and George go to the end of the town and select a splendid new ochre and white bowl of glazed earthenware. This article Yanni and the children carry triumphantly along the whole crowded length of the *plateia*, George having shamefully slipped around the corner to talk to a friend.

The progress of the little party is slow. Every few yards somebody stops Yanni to examine the bowl, to ask its price, to tap it carefully to test its strength. The children obligingly regale the curious with a full history of the awful accident that befell the old one. George sidles furtively down the alley beside the coffee-house of Manolis Klonaris and slips neatly through the door, just in time to assist Yanni in the task of uprooting the old and installing the new.

Mercifully, my only role is to light incense in a tin lid and keep waving it about that end of the house where work is in progress. They emerge finally, panting but triumphant. George is very pale. He has the look of a man who has passed through an unforgettable experience. In a weak voice he asks for some *very* hot water and the bottle of Dettol. After one look at the sad remains I decide to keep the incense burning.

The problem now, of course, is what to do with it.

'It is a pity,' says George, 'that they have no museum here.'

Will the garbage man take it away? Here a matter of pride is involved, and embarrassment. It is true that the garbage man has a donkey with a wooden box roped to its saddle, but it is not a very large wooden box, and the garbage man himself is a very small man, lost to finer points of judgement.

'*Po-po-po-po-po!*' murmurs Yanni reassuringly. I have a queer feeling that time has unaccountably slipped. This is where Yanni, in the role of the shy Mister John, came in. '*Paithi mou,*' he grins, using the affectionate, tolerant 'my child.' 'What do you think the sea is for — the *thalassa*? I will tell you what we do. When it is dark we will hurry down the stairs, very quickly and quietly, and we will throw it in the sea. The sea is a very efficient garbage disposal. It is the Kalymnian system.'

So it is arranged. I am to go downstairs in advance to make sure that all is clear on the *plateia*. When I give the signal George and Yanni will rush across to the sea railings and pitch hard and strong.

It is deemed advisable to wait until late at night, after the *tavernas* have closed.

The two of them, holding the awful object between them, lurk behind the street door at the foot of the stairs while I stroll nonchalantly out into the square. There is a moon, but it is not all *that* bright. There are four divers singing softly together down near the war memorial, and the duty policeman is strolling slowly across the *plateia* midway between the salt trees and the sea.

'Wait a bit!' I hiss urgently. Unfortunately I have spoken in English, and Yanni interprets this as the all-clear. He rushes impetuously into the street, dragging George and the burden after him.

George sees the policeman from the corner of his eye and tries to draw back, but it is too late. In any event, Yanni is the stronger of the two. For the second time language brings our downfall. At the edge of the railing George desperately pants 'one, two, three!' and heaves. But Yanni, out of synchronisation, is gasping *'ena, thio, trial!'* His heave comes a fraction later.

The loathsome relic slips from their grasp and breaks between them on the street with a crash that must be heard on Kos.

There is a moment of dreadful, disbelieving silence. Then the two of them are streaking for the door.

The policeman has begun to run, shouting what is surely the Greek equivalent of 'stop, thief!' Windows are cracking up all along the square, people are bounding from doorways and materialising magically from the shadows beneath the trees. The song of the divers has ended abruptly. They pound in full cry towards us.

In the confusing pattern of the shadows we are not seen. Everyone is shouting at once, and the policeman has grabbed the nearest bystander and is questioning him accusingly. In the pale, chequered moonlight all the square is aflutter with explanatory hands.

Safe inside the house, George and Yanni are leaning against the balcony door, rocking with helpless laughter. The policeman has marched off into the night, looking a little angry and foolish. For a while the crowd remains standing in a mystified circle around the scattered fragments of porcelain.

Two small boys at last kick the pieces into the sea.

'You see!' says Yanni triumphantly. 'It is in the *thalassa*. This, George, is the Kalymnian system.'

8

We had been on the island for a month before any mail got through to us, so our first postal delivery was a huge one: letters and one or two unpaid bills, magazines and newspapers sent to keep us 'in touch', and an enormous brown paper envelope stuffed with Christmas cards whose tinselled robins, half-timbered cottages, blazing yule logs and sequined bunches of mistletoe gained the curious charm of period pieces for being three weeks late and half a world away. The bright and glittering pictures completely captivated our Kalymnian friends, who carefully carried off the prancing reindeer, Flemish madonnas, startled Magi and Stars of Bethlehem left over after we had decorated our own damp walls with selected prints.

Yanni, evincing an unsuspected streak of audacity, chose an abstract and personalised card designed by one of our more clever London friends. The card depicted a two-headed Santa Claus whose navel could be pulled open to reveal a gin bottle inscribed with an invitation to attend a Chelsea studio orgy long since drawn to its riotous close. This, with a watercolour reproduction of central Australia and a glossy photograph of the Sydney Harbour bridge, he bore triumphantly to his little house in the alleys behind Agios Christos and tacked it to the blue wall between a Swiss oleograph and a highly coloured

picture of a Paris *exposition* of the 'seventies. I have no doubt
it will remain there to mystify his descendants for generations
to come.

Our own Kalymnian Christmas had of necessity been a
makeshift business —

'But *Mum*!'

Martin, wearing only a very small pair of patched blue shorts
and carrying a string of minute fish threaded through their gills,
had just arrived with Apostoli and Georgouli to make more bait.
All three of them are the colour of leather and are rimed white
with salt about the ears and eyebrows. Now that Martin's hair is
cropped in the Kalymnian manner nothing but his blue eyes and
still slightly hesitant and pedantic Greek distinguishes him from
his two best friends.

'What is it, Marty?'

'Why are you writing down that stuff about its being
makeshift?'

'Well, I only mean that we had to concoct everything
ourselves, the decorations and the crib and everything. We
couldn't buy anything in shops, the way we did in London.'

'Oh, *I* remember...' He stands by the table, twirling the
string of fish, and pensively rubs one bare foot up and down his
leg. His expression is vague and melancholy, his eyes misty with
distance. Seeing what? I wonder ... lights smeared in the cold
white air like fuming stars? churned seas of cellophane where
glittering marvels erupt and sink? flaming trees as tall as spires?
globes of ruby, sapphire, emerald?

'Did we buy our cribs in a shop too?'

'We never had a crib in London. There never seemed time to
make one, somehow.'

'Well, it was a jolly good crib here.' The bemused, wistful
look has cleared. He gives the fish string a little confident flip.
'Everyone made his cross in front of it just like the real Mary
and Jesus in church.'

I have a feeling that this is important. Whether one believes
or does not that a Christ child was born in a stable at Bethlehem,
it is only the stable that brings us together at Christmas, not the

grotesque torrent of expensive toys, gin-and-turkey clubs and harried shop assistants.

In Kalymnos one touches again the immediacy and the dramatic excitement of Christmas, for Christmas begins on the evening of December the twenty-fourth. There are no advertising campaigns, no high-pressure salesmanship, no hysterical reminders of the number of shopping days left — there is nothing to sell or to buy. At three o'clock on Christmas morning we had stumbled downstairs with lighted lamps to answer the urgent knocking on the street door. Out of the wildly pealing bells, the sea-smelling darkness and the glitter of innumerable candles on the mountains Manolis had swum golden into the lamplight, his arms outstretched and his gaunt face queerly smiling, like Scrooge irradiated. 'My dear brother and sister,' he said. 'Christ is born!'

'Well, Marty, I'm glad you weren't disappointed in our first Greek Christmas.'

'What? Oh, no. It was jolly good.' But it has slipped away, the clanging bells and the cheap little crib, the four of us climbing up to Saint Nikolas from the dark sea and the quiet ships, the dawn pricked all about with moving candles.

Outside now the sun is clear and brilliant, the sun of July. On the long pier fifty naked and glistening little boys bake in the sun or plop into the cool green water where two months ago the *aktaramathes* rode in coloured ranks.

'Did you know, Mum,' Martin says impressively, 'that Georgouli's got some fish *poison!*'

Our letters and London newspapers and magazines from New York touched us with a growing sense of unreality. The events they described seemed as remote and fantastic as the machinations of the green-faced Mekon on the front page of the children's comic that arrived in the newspaper bundle. The politics and scandal of Fleet Street seemed as credible.

We have our own newspapers. There is Stathis, who hobbles slowly along the waterfront two or three times a day, gnarled and bent as the stick of olive root he leans on. Stathis cries shipping schedules and local information in a slow and sonorous chant as dignified and impressive as a *Times* leader. Advertising is handled by Dionyssos, a crippled diver with a moustache like a great black bar beneath his nose and a rakish tilt to his seaman's cap. Dionyssos still dives in the summer, but in the winter months he is hung all over with tasselled tablecloths and ladies' clothing hooked by coat hangers to his collar and sleeves. He bawls out his copy from the middle of the street with a salesman's fervour. His is the definitive form of what has come to be called public relations. 'Walk up! Walk up!' he begs the *gorgonas*, and the *gorgonas* obediently walk up and test the quality of his jumpers and petticoats and headscarves with horny thumbs and forefingers.

Foreign news is always obtainable at the coffee-house of Pantalés, a poor man's philosopher who looks like the later Rembrandt self portraits and makes the most fragrant and delicious coffee I have ever tasted on a tin can with three embers of charcoal inside it. Like all good foreign editors Pantalés is sometimes overwhelmed by the madness of the world. When this happens he brings his two rickety tables and eight chairs from the pavement and locks himself in with the tin can, the coffee cups and the ranks of empty, dusty bottles that carry rare and famous labels — sad relics of the time when Pantalés kept the finest bar in Kalymnos. For a week or a month he sits inside the shuttered shop and drinks morosely all day and half the night among the ghostly shadows of Courvoisier and Mumm and Haig, the hanging bay leaves, the yellowed copies of the Athens newspapers. And his patrons see the great padlock on the blue door and shrug and smile and go away. But in between these Homeric bouts his comments on the follies of mankind are intelligent and as lively as the big cockroaches that scuttle around beneath his tables. Pantalés is the interpreter of all that happens in foreign parts, the mythographer of his native island, the philologist whose word on semantics is always final and irrefutable. With us at first he commented without words, since our Greek was negligible and our pronunciation beneath his discriminating consideration, but his miming was marvellous. Using the top of the table, twigs from the overhanging salt tree, spoons, coffee cups and spilled pools of water, he would explain the significance of Bulganin's rise and Malenkov's decline, or the Cyprian problem, or Churchill's mistake about the Dardanelles in 1915.

From Stathis, Dionyssos and Pantalés we learned all we needed to know about outside events. Even the realisation of how little we needed to know left no residue of regret for the years we had wasted worrying about the morning's headlines or the evening bulletin from the radio. We had no wish to go back to it.

We had by this time surrendered our passports and an incredible number of little grey glaring photographs to the police, who gave us in exchange stamped and signed registration cards that entitled us to stay on the island for six months longer.

('Be happy! Be happy!' George used to mutter as we scurried for the tenth time between the police station and the mayor's office to fill out yet another batch of forms and pay yet another fifty *drachmae* for official stamps. The consul in London might never have heard of Kafka, but 'They' are not to be overlooked once you are actually in Greece. Or perhaps it is that there is a great deal of difference between 'tourist' and 'alien'. I had never been an alien before, anywhere in the world.)

But if our life on Kalymnos was not the Greek idyll we had envisioned in London, at least we were learning to relax a little, to say *then pirasi* and *avrio* almost as nonchalantly as Manolis. And we were working at the novel steadily and easily. If we had had only ourselves to worry about I think that even so early we would have been perfectly content. But there were the children.

In London it had been easy enough to theorise on the advantages the children would gain from living on a Greek island. And the theories were sound enough, as theories go. I still believe that city life, and particularly flat life, with its physical restrictions and the necessity for constant adult supervision, is not good for children. All the progressive education in the world, all the cunningly designed nursery toys and handicraft kits, cannot compensate for the loss of a child's first right to make his own discoveries. It saddened me that at the age of seven Martin could give me an interesting and lucid account of the life cycle of a tree but couldn't climb one. Tree climbing is discouraged in Kensington Gardens. In London it had been simple to say that I did not want my children to become over-stimulated, over-sophisticated, over-educated asphalt and playing-area products. My own Australian childhood had been wild and free. And although the details and even the names of the games we played then were lost to me, I had never lost the knowledge that was woven into those games — a free child's certain knowledge of the limitless possibilities of the human body, the limitless aspirations of the human soul.

But it is one thing to grow up in freedom and another thing entirely to be thrown into it. Looking down from the window at Martin and Shane banging and shrieking self-consciously in the middle of a group of Kalymnian children, I realised with a sense of shame and alarm that they didn't know *how* to play. How could they know? All their play had been nursery games with blocks and toy soldiers and dolls and building sets and electric trains, their outdoor recreation restricted by the traffic of the Bayswater Road, the English climate, the by-laws of Kensington Gardens, and the amount of time I could spare to supervise them. Now the tight nursery walls had expanded to the limits of the sea and the sky and the mountains, and they were lost and uncertain in the vastness of it all. They were, moreover, quite incapable of understanding or communicating with their playfellows, and contrary to everything I had expected, they resisted the language stubbornly and took refuge in lordliness or exhibitionism. Shane, who is normally the sunniest and most affectionate of little girls, became surly and defiant. Martin's shoulders drooped and he was given to spasms of uncontrollable panic. It was obviously a condition that time would remedy, but in the beginning they needed love and understanding and patience as they had never needed these things in their lives before.

Then too, the poverty of their playfellows bewildered them. Poverty, in the deep Greek sense of the word, was something of which they had had no experience. There had been nothing in their lives to prepare them for a world where children had neither coats nor shoes nor toys to play with, and very often not enough to eat.

'Well, I can't ask the Kicker to our party,' I overheard Shane saying to Martin one morning just before Christmas.

'But why, Shaney?' Martin asked. 'She doesn't kick *us*. The egg-shaped ones are the ones she kicks. I'd ask her if I were you, because if you don't she might kick us too.'

'It isn't because she *kicks*', Shane said, then added with devastating simplicity, 'she's only got a raggy dress, Marty. How could she come to a *party*?' In Shane's rather extensive experience of parties an organdy dress, rosebud wreath and dancing slippers had been as imperative as pink ice-cream and balloons.

Later, tidying the window-ledge where their toys were piled in the absence of any other furniture, I saw that Martin's treasured soldiers were missing. Questioned, he admitted rather worriedly to having given them all away, together with a box of a hundred coloured pencils.

'But I thought you loved your soldiers and your pencils more than anything, Martin.'

'Oh, but I *do*, Mum,' he said, and burst into regretful tears. He had divided the soldiers and the pencils, he explained, among Yo-yo and Apostoli and Miches and Vassilis the cigarette boy and the boy Dimitri who sold peanuts and one of the egg-shaped ones. 'They didn't have *any* toys, Mum. Not *any*!'

Gradually all the toys they had brought from London went the same way, some in gifts and some in bribes. That they afterwards regretted their generosity, or cowardice, was natural enough, particularly as they were still suffering under the misapprehension that such things were as easily replaceable as they always had been. But the periods of regret were very brief. They soon discovered they could have better games with five stones or skipping ropes or home-made kites, and there was the sea to play in and boats to crawl around on, and fishhooks to be strung on thin gut lines and toy boats to be hammered out of old paraffin tins. And there were crabs and sea urchins to be looked for on the rocks, and shells and coloured pebbles to be brought back and stored in jars and boxes. Gradually the word 'toy' disappeared altogether from their vocabularies. By then they could speak Greek and go barefoot and have patches in their trousers. Their nursery had become the world.

There was one other lesson though that took longer to learn. When we were all invited to one of the poor Kalymnian houses for a meal it was agony to have to sit and watch them pushing around on their plates a great piece of squid, slithery with oil, their faces expressing all too plainly that terrible inward struggle between nausea and politeness, or trying desperately to avoid having to take a thick slab of black bread generously spread with the lumpy, evil-smelling fat that passes here for butter.

'Take it, *take it*!' our hostess would urge them in bewilderment. 'It is good. It is *butter*!' Behind her her own children would stand with hungry eyes fixed on the delicacy. They had probably eaten nothing all day but dry bread so that my children, the strangers, could be offered 'butter.'

In nothing is the cruel poverty of this island revealed more clearly than in the diet of its inhabitants. In exactly the same way as the tree is the yardstick of natural beauty — 'ah, it is a beautiful place; it has trees!' — food has become the measure of all sociology and economics. America and Australia are spoken of always in terms of food. A migrant writes from a works project in New South Wales to say that they eat four times a day, and this startling information is carried all over the town and discussed for days. 'No work, no food!' is an expression heard as frequently as the half-despairing, half-ironic, 'Ah, it passes the time!' from the listless coffee-house gamblers who have no work and no escape. It is perfectly polite to greet a comparative stranger and to ask immediately what he has eaten for his midday meal or to question your neighbour on what she intends to cook for supper.

For most of the islanders the staple diet is beans, macaroni, potatoes and bread, with fish if the price is cheap or plain boiled rice with oil. Meat is a dish for feast days. The basic frugality of the poor can be expressed simply in the abstention from meat. Meat costs twenty-five *drachmae* a kilo. The average wage of the worker, when there *is* work for him, is twenty-five *drachmae* a day — a twelve-or fourteen-hour working day with no break for meals.

This frugality is inevitably reflected on the shelves of the stores. At first trying to find something to cook was a nightmare. Apart from the innumerable bottles of Samian cherry brandy, *strega,* crème de menthe, curaçao, banana liqueur and apricot brandy, to say nothing of the ubiquitous *ouzo,* which filled half the shelves of the grocers' shops (God knows why, because these drinks are not cheap) there was little to buy except the basic articles of Kalymnian diet: flour, rice, oil, olives, beans of several varieties, macaroni in a dozen different shapes and sizes and an occasional tin of some 'luxury' commodity — marmalade or Dutch butter or condensed milk or corned beef.

The market, an ugly, crumbling pseudo-Venetian building constructed near the fishing wharves behind the cathedral during the Italian occupation, did not offer much more, although like all near-Oriental markets it was a delight to the eye. The oranges and tangerines glowed, the walls were festooned with garlands of dried vineleaves and nubbly corms of garlic threaded on yellow straw, and glossy green peppers spilled over into trays of silvery onions. I wanted to bury my face in the baskets of fragrant lemons or stand and stare at the old potato seller with her skirts hooked back over a striped petticoat or at the greenstalk boy lolling by the broken fountain with his basket of gleaming mackerel. Yet, finished admiring, what was there after all that I could put in my basket to make two sustaining meals for four people?

We were victims of the natural rhythm of the seasons — the realisation that there *were* seasons had long been blunted by the chilled chamber and the deep freeze, by the preserving pan and the refrigerated cargo ship, so the limitations of the changing year came as something of a shock. Here on Kalymnos fruits and vegetables are seasonal, as God doubtless intended them to be. We ate salad for a few weeks, then suddenly there was no more lettuce and cucumbers were 'in.' The cucumbers disappeared a day or two before the first tomatoes arrived. It was impossible ever to eat a salad that had cucumber *and* tomato *and* lettuce *and* onion. I have asked Kalymnian women why they did not buy fruit and vegetables when they were plentiful and cheap (tomatoes and apricots and pears at a penny a pound) and preserve them for winter. They stared at me blankly. I drew pictures of simple preserving jars. They exclaimed with delight and carried the sketches off to show their friends. We made no further progress.

'But there are no plums in winter,' they would say in mystified tones. 'Oranges and tangerines, yes, but no plums. If God had intended us to eat plums in winter, He would have put them on the trees then.'

Even fish is not so plentiful as you might expect on an Aegean island which supports a moderately large fishing industry. Again poverty is the reason. Here nobody can afford to pay a price for fish that ensures a reasonable margin of profit for the fisherman. He packs his catch in ice and sends it to the Piraeus market. Our children, in any case, with sharp memories of the soggy skate served at school lunches and the stench and swarming flies of London's open fishstalls, still had an understandable revulsion for fish in all forms.

Once a week, sometimes twice, there were a few bloody carcasses strung from hooks over the wooden chopping blocks in the *agora* annex. We always knew when the meat would be there, because the animals were driven to the slaughterhouse right across the *plateia* under our balcony, and we soon learned to appraise the quality of the squealing pigs, the exquisite little tan and white kids with tiny nubs of horns and sharp little rapping hooves, the scraggy grey ewes with their curious yellow eyes, the arrogant mountain rams with horns curled back like convoluted shells, the lean, sinewy steers that sometimes took an hour or more of tugging and tail-twisting by eagerly assisting small boys to pass across the *plateia*. By evening the same animals would be hung on hooks, having passed again down the *plateia* on open wooden mulecarts that dripped scarlet on the street. A small boy rode nonchalantly astride the carcasses, and the mule was decked with blue beads and bells. If you wanted meat you hurried after the mulecarts. There was never any choice about which part of the animal you were going to have, no nonsense about sirloin or T-bone or cutlet or haunch. A piece was hacked off, bones, fat, sinews, tripes and all, and handed to you still warm and bloody. You took it home and did your own finer butchery.

Although my kitchen at first seemed to me as primitive as a fire stick, I soon realised from the envy of my neighbours that it was in fact the Kalymnian equivalent of an all-electric. I had *two* charcoal grates! And a kerosene burner as well! It is very rare for any house here to have more than one grate. This may be inside the house or built outside, supported on a cube of whitewashed brick. Often it is only a tin can with holes punched in it, but it serves to cook meals for a family of ten. People in more comfortable circumstances use a primus stove — but only one, and with a single burner, like the one in the house of the *raptis* at Kos. It doesn't seem to have occurred to anybody yet that with two burners you can cook two things at once. In Greece — or at least in Kalymnos — you cook one dish and then cook another while the first is getting cold. After a while you grow accustomed to eating your fish or meat or vegetables lukewarm or cold. At least that is what other people tell me. I haven't abandoned all efforts to serve hot meals.

Many of the houses have outside bread ovens, crude domes of whitewashed clay in which bread is baked after the ovens are heated with blazing bundles of gorse carried down from the mountains. They are exactly the same as the primitive ovens unearthed in the ancient city of Damos, contemporaneous with the Mycenae of Agamemnon. Stoves as we understand them are unknown. It is impossible to find even one of those clumsy old-fashioned wood ranges that were almost obsolete in small Australian country towns when I was a child.

On feast days or the rare occasions when a woman can afford a dish more complicated, and therefore more expensive, than the interminable macaroni and beans, she prepares the food at home and then carries it to the commercial bakers' ovens, where she can have her dish cooked for two *drachmae*. Then she carries it home, sometimes a mile or more, and quite possibly to the top of a mountain, so by the time she sets it down on the table it is quite cold.

There were times, stirring the one pot balanced precariously on a few embers of charcoal or gingerly lighting the kerosene cooker that had a temperamental knack of blowing up in my face (for weeks I was devoid of both eyebrows and eyelashes!) when I remembered with a deep sense of unreality the black and white enamel of my London kitchen, the flick of the oven regulator and the soft humming of the big refrigerator in the corner, the smell of the soap whirling in the washing machine, the crimson handles of the matched set of beaters and mixers and slicers and lifters, the graded aluminium saucepans, the pyrex dishes and the wooden serving platters I had pressed upon friends whose kitchens were already loaded with similar equipment, the

Georgian sherry glasses and the silver entrée dishes, the clever coloured plates from Heal's, the considerable remains of the Wedgwood Moss Rose placings I had presented as a parting gift to the charlady … How had I ever found use for it all?

In fact there are hundreds of good dishes to be made with the available Kalymnian materials and a single charcoal grate. Sevasti gently but firmly began to teach me Greek cooking. We began with *fasolia*, a bean dish with tomato purée, celery, onion, oil and garlic, progressed to *dolmadhes*, rice and a little meat wrapped in vineleaves, and *kucha*, fresh thick beans cooked with mountain herbs. We made wonderful spaghetti and sauce dishes. And as I began to learn the language I was able to bully the butcher into giving me better cuts of meat, so sometimes we could have tiny meatballs or stewed lamb or kid with bay leaves and fresh onions no larger than marbles.

To my intense relief the children began to develop voracious appetites, and even got around to thinking that fresh fish fried golden in oil pressed from the groves a mile down the road was a satisfactory breakfast food. And a farmer in a wide hat came to call every morning, treading light as a cat on his high, soft goatskin boots, bringing little earthenware bowls of yoghurt made from creamy sheep's milk. Even the plebian pumpkin could be transformed into sweet little yellow cakes, fried in oil for the children's tea. And there came the day, proud and inevitable, when Martin took the Sunday dinner to the baker's oven, carrying the big tin dish on his cropped head as if it were a crown.

A rare wave of nostalgia led him one day to urge me to make Cornish pasties, a request so astonishing that I acceded to it. By some singular stroke of fortune they were magnificently successful, filling Sevasti with amazement and admiration. She hurried home and ran up a batch herself. So did Angela in the next house but one. By the following Saturday morning there were a dozen trays of Cornish pasties in the baker's oven. If some day an anthropologist bases a learned treatise on this curious aspect of Kalymnian diet, bringing in the Amber Route and Phoenician tin trade and early Greek migration to the Hyperborean Isles, I shall be content. It is my only culinary triumph.

We also rediscovered seafood, an appetite quite lost in London, where the fishstalls are probably the most unhygienic and revolting in the civilised world and where oysters cost a fortune. We have never developed that degree of indigenous relish which enables Yanni to eat live crabs and sea urchins, wriggling spikes and all, but we have come to have a taste for octopus in any of the hundred dishes you can make from it; and *fooskas*, a strange, black, hairy sea fruit that the divers bring up — the meat is black and crimson, and you eat it with oil and lemon; and the strange-looking *pinas*, pale, mussel-like shellfish, which grow to the length of your arm and, like the clam, can take a diver's fingers or hand off if he is not careful how he grabs. The meat of the *pinas* is fried and tastes rather like very tender and slightly salty liver. Then there are *palamethes*, a sort of mackerel plentiful off the Anatolian coast, sliced and grilled like steak and served hot with oil and lemon juice or cold with a thick garlic sauce that will match anything the Cordon Bleu can produce; and the tiny crisp *smarithes* which you eat whole — head, bones, tail and all.

'Oh God for a Press Club turbot!' George murmurs contentedly, dabbing the oil from his chin. 'Or one of those nice grey shepherd's pies! Pass the *palamethes*, there's a good girl, and I'll write you an Iliad!'

9

As the weeks passed and our problems were solved one by one — or became so familiar that we could live with them with a degree of indifference — the book began to make its own pace. The story was all around us. We were living in it. We sipped morning coffees with our characters, and at night we sat with them in the *tavernas*, sharing copper beakers of *retzina* and platters of *barbunia* (a Mediterranean form of red mullet), that exquisite gold-pink fish that was painted as a decorative motif on the walls of the palace of Minos at Cnossus four thousand years ago, that was worked into the beautiful early Greek mosaics of Kos, now preserved in the museum at Rhodes, that was pictured in gold thread on the copes of Byzantine patriarchs and threaded into the primitive Aegean textiles of the early Middle Ages, now the joy of the Benaki Museum in Athens.

It seems irreverent to jab a fork into that delicate, shimmering pink shape. This is the food that sustained Daedalus, dreaming of labyrinths and wings and brazen bulls, that nourished the charms of Ariadne and was brought, flanked by double axes, on dishes of beaten gold to the table of Minos. Yet jab one does, greedily and to hell with reverence. The white flesh is delicious, and we sop our bread in the golden pools of oil and lick our fingers after.

I have never tried to find out how many *tavernas* there are in Kalymnos, but in this town where night life is largely focused on a 'sailor ashore' trade there must be a great many. Four of them either for their atmosphere or picturesqueness could be classified as four-star *tavernas*. The rest are for the most part dingy and smoky little boxes of rooms lined with big barrels in wooden racks. They shatter the peace of the twisty little alleyways with metallic *bouzoukia* music blared forth cacophonously from the same few scratched phonograph records that are played over and over again.

In the *tavernas* generally nothing is served but *retzina*, though in the summer a concession might be made to keep a few bottles of Greek beer in a pail of lukewarm water. As the exuberant Kalymnian hospitality makes it impossible *not* to drink, it becomes a matter of whether or not one likes *retzina*. *Retzina* is an acquired taste. One either abominates it or becomes a passionate devotee.

Retzina is almost certainly the oldest wine on earth, and quite probably the cheapest. It takes its name from the pine resin mixed with the wine when it is ready to go into the casks, a fact which drew from a medieval French traveller the caustic comment that the Greeks, unlike the rest of the world, pressed their wine not from grapes but from pine forests. The basic wine before it is resinated is almost always a still white wine not unlike a rather light Moselle or Chablis. Kalymnos produces a small amount of red *retzina* known as *kokkinelli*, slightly less resinated than the white, and which is wonderful to drink in summer when the normal *retzina* is inclined to be too heavy. Unfortunately it is not easy to come by. The addition of the resin gives to the wine what is at first a very peculiar taste — I gagged on my first glass, sipped with Borgia caution at the second and became an addict with the third — but adherents of the cult swear emphatically that it is the resin that transforms the wine into a virtual elixir. It will make you happy, keep you young, enable you to live to a hundred. It will never give you a hangover (this much is true), and any doctor will tell you of its beneficial properties: for the legs, the eyes, the joints, the liver, the kidneys, the heart, the spleen, the lungs, the nerves. 'How's your health?' old Leonidas, the vendor of honey cakes and sweet syrups, asks

87

as his normal greeting. 'Take the *retzina*. For the *organismós* there is nothing like the *retzina*!'

The practice of adding resin to wine is thousands of years old. The discovery of wine is attributed to the god Dionysus, the place generally held to be Eleutherae, on the slopes of Mount Cithaeron. The story of the god's strange wanderings and the later mystic rites of the Dionysian cult were presumed to symbolise the spread of the wine cult, in supercession to the Thracian beer cult, across Europe, Asia and North Africa. In fact it is more likely that wine was first made in Crete — the Cretan grapes and wines are still famous — and exported to Greece in wine jars around the beginning of the second millennium before Christ. Lacking the knowledge of maturing and preserving wine in wooden casks, these early wine makers added pine resin as a way to keep the wine fresh aboard ships. Theseus sailing to Crete or Jason taking the *Argo* to Colchis in search of the Golden Fleece, would have drunk *retzina* probably no different from the *retzina* we drink today. It was the drink of Odysseus, of the men who sacked Troy, of the victors at Salamis. Wine jars 2,600 years old have been brought up from beneath the sea still bearing traces of the resin with which they had been impregnated.

The practice of resination has another value also. The characteristic astringency it imparts to the wine counteracts the oily heaviness of most Greek food. Moreover, there is a particular significance attached to the drinking of *retzina* which applies to no other beverage. Each glassful is a toast, with the glasses all tapped together ceremoniously. In a large party the glass-tapping can become quite a labour. You can avoid it without losing politeness merely by tapping the base of the glass against the table. Frequently, and in Kalymnos almost always, one glass of *retzina* is always deliberately spilled on the floor as a sort of libation. Why this is done I have no idea. I have asked many Kalymnian men. They smile sheepishly, shake their heads and shrug. They do not know why ... it has always been done. Obviously it is some sort of appeasement, a lingering atavism related to some ancient and long-forgotten ritual.

*

The *taverna* we have come to like best is Anthony Skeftarios', which lies at the end of a blind alley off one of the cobbled side streets twisting away from Agios Christos. It is a square, uncompromising room washed a harsh blue with a harsh red trim which comes off on your clothing if you lean against the wall. It contains twelve small, solid tables spread with clean black-and-white-checked cloths. The floor is bare board, well scrubbed but full of knotholes that make pitfalls for chair legs and frequently trap the unwary drinker. There are no adornments on the walls, except for a not-very-good pencil sketch of Skeftarios and a calendar which always marks the correct date. There is a green counter with a slab of slate let into the top where Skeftarios chalks down your score. And on the counter stands a tray of glasses and a thirty-kilo wicker-covered jar which is replenished as the need requires from the larger and more pretentious *taverna* of Tasos Zordos, just around the corner.

Zordos' big *taverna* enchanted me at first with its panorama of blue barrels piled to the roof — sixty-four of them, all numbered — and the sawdust on the floor and the pattern of vineleaves painted on the walls and the loud twangling tunes scraped from an ancient gramophone with a curly horn. I thought then, and still do, that if Zordos could transport his *taverna* intact to any of the cities where the idle and sophisticated sigh for the simple life and pay ready money for the vicarious titillation of drinking like the peasant or the fisherman, he would make a fortune. So would fat Mikailis. His *taverna* is picturesque in a different way. Like Skeftarios', it is in a brightly coloured alleyway close to the sea. When you turn down it you can hear the waves soughing under the gratings beneath your feet. Beneath its buckling ceiling of pasted-together sheets of paper the *taverna* is like a huge vaulted cave. It is furnished with the old high-backed, crudely carved benches and long refectory tables that belonged to the grandmother of Mikailis' wife and came to Mikailis as part of the marriage *prika*. The third of the spectacular *tavernas* sits beneath an enormous mulberry tree which in summer must be worth tens of thousands of *drachmae* to the patron, a genial and gigantic Turk named Theodoros Saris, who still smokes the Turkish *ngaliyeh* or hubble-bubble pipe. Saris is the authority on Turkish singing and, with an admirable tolerance, decorates the wall of his *taverna* with lithographs of the Greek heroes of the war of liberation against the Turks.

Yet more and more frequently in those early weeks we found ourselves passing the alley that turns down to Mikailis' establishment and not going quite far enough to come to Zordos' place or to reach the mulberry tree of the Turkish giant. The picturesque palls. The gramophone is, after all, a nuisance if you want to talk; Mikailis' cavern is too cold, the lavatory by the door stinks, and the divers, for some reason, never go there. Skeftarios' is the divers' *taverna* almost as inviolably as Saint Stephanos is their patron saint.

Skeftarios' is like the Greek landscape — bare and innocent and strangely stimulating. It can all be taken in at a glance — the walls, the counter, the broken floor, the two windows that look into the clean kitchen where the twisted, solid trunk of a very old vine thrusts up through the floor, leans against the cheaply papered walls among the shining pots and pans, pokes through the roof, and hangs its thick clusters of purple grapes across the trellis outside. Skeftarios' wife, Golden Anna — huge and grey as a hippopotamus — stands in front of the primus stove in a cloud of aromatic smoke, deftly turning the *barbunia*. The round bare arm of quiet Katerina chops ribbons of lettuce on a wooden board. There is nothing else. Yet here you eat better, drink better, think better and talk better than any place I know. You are moved to music and poetry and dreams.

The top left-hand corner is invariably annexed to the giants: Captain Miches, who runs three diving boats and has a body like a tree, a beautiful, battered plug-ugly face and the eyes of a child; his *colazáris* Mikailis, who is even bigger than Miches and handsome, with the pure, austere beauty of a face on an old coin. (Mikailis could wear bronze greaves and a helmet with a red-dyed horsehair plume as fittingly as he wears his sea boots and seaman's cap — and if his wild drinking and sometimes tiresomely childish prankishness seem to assort oddly with the pure, stern line of his profile one must remember that Achilles was sulky, Paris vain, Ajax stupid, Odysseus sly and Nestor nothing but a bore.) Pavlos Roditis, the huge cousin of the huge Golden Anna, who has a belly like a sack of meal and a voice like the blast of a conchshell; Anthony Mavrikaikas, the mayor, entitled to a place at the table by his size alone. All the largest, toughest and least inhibited of the divers who sail with Captain Miches are at the corner table. It is the corner of Homeric appetites and Homeric jests, of huge, aching belly laughs and belches that sound like volcanoes erupting. Through the kitchen window Golden Anna and Katerina pass an endless chain of gigantic bowls — lobsters, *fooskas*, lamb stewed with potatoes, *barbunia*, yellow omelettes, green hummocks of salad, *palamethes*, cheese. Skeftarios, dangling an unlighted cigarette from his top lip, phlegmatically fills and refills the ranks of copper beakers and goes round to Tasos Zordos to replenish the wicker jar.

'Crazy men!' mutters Georgios the merchant, who has wandered in wispily, whistling Léhar. (One is momentarily surprised that it is a figure so diminutive and frail, not Rabelais or Falstaff come to join them.) But he drifts to the giants' corner like a thin blown thistle, disappearing for a moment like Jack hiding in the giant's kitchen. He emerges again, his white bobbing head half concealed under a big black seaman's cap. And the frail, sugary strains of Léhar trail off into the roared chorus of *Psara-poula*, the sponge divers' own song, which is bellowed to the accompaniment of banging beakers and sloshing glasses. One feels inevitably that the curtain is about to fall on Act One.

'Crazy music!' Caralis protests happily, blissfully taking up the second verse. But down in the old men's corner, diagonally opposite, the other Georgios, the old man with the sad clown's face, grimaces and appeals to us mutely. This modern muck! his long hands say. He is a very tall old man, jointed loosely like a rag doll that has lost half its stuffing. His sad blue eyes slope down at the corners. His companions are the three other old

91

men (the four of them together muster an eventful two hundred and eighty-two years) who have out of their own venerability established a corner of Skeftarios' as sacrosanct, as inviolate, as the corner of the giants.

Here, sad and quiet, sits white-haired Anthonis Pandalis — *Capitano* Anthonis. He is seventy-two and was once a sponge captain with a boat of his own and a fine young boy who was the best diver of them all. But the boy was killed in the fighting in Korea, the boat has another captain, and old Anthonis sells cigarettes from a wooden box with beautiful little coloured drawings of sponge boats pasted inside the lid.

The chair next to the *capitano* is always reserved for Nicko — cynical, jovial, villainous Nicko, proud possessor of the biggest belly on the island, who fought the Turks through Thrace and Macedonia and loved a French girl in New Orleans. He always carries inside his shirt crushed carnation heads and pink roses and green, heady sprigs of *vassilikos* which, as Golden Anna explains (she being the *taverna*'s final authority on all things pious), derives its royal name from having sprouted from the cross of Christ in the ashpit where Helena found it.

The fourth chair in the corner is always occupied by Emmanuele Manglis, who at the age of sixty-six is the youngest of the quartet but looks older than any of them. He is aware of this, and accepts the fact equably. 'The diving life,' he explains, 'adds ten or fifteen years to the looks of any man.' He was a diver for twenty-five years and was brutally crippled: it did not prevent him from being the captain for many years of all the Kalymnian divers and the acknowledged authority on the lore and history and techniques of the hazardous profession.

His cousin Anthony Manglis represents, in a sense, the other side of the Kalymnian coin. He symbolises, as it were, the steady element of the island. He stands for the mercantile, the prosperous, the respectable, the progressive, the reliable factors. He is a man of considerable wealth and great commercial talent, handling the very considerable Vouvalis estates as well as his own, merchandising sponges in the markets of the world. He is a friendly and pleasant man, charming, cultivated and able.

Kiriakos, the young farmer who manages his rich citrus estate at Vathy, swears that there is no finer man in all the world to work for. Yet one finds oneself inevitably lingering on the absolute separateness of the lives of these two branches of the family. It is, in a way, the perfect example of the great schism which ruthlessly divides all the life of Kalymnos. Has Anthony Manglis, I wonder, ever drunk *retzina* at a corner table in Skeftarios'?

For all his poverty and pain Emmanuele Manglis still has what is sometimes called background. Sitting at the corner table with the other old men, twirling his splendid snowy moustache, his manners as beautiful and as courtly as his language, he will tell the ancient legend of the desertion of Ariadne on Naxos with the eager, bright-eyed enthusiasm of a young poet. His courtesy is unfailing, his fund of stories inexhaustible. His charm can transform rough *retzina* into château-bottled Laffitte and the checked gingham tablecloth into damask.

On the old men's table there is never more than a meagre half *oka* of *retzina* and a small plate of cheese or olives. They are all pitifully poor. It fascinates me to see one of the demigods descend from the Olympian corner to join them, bringing, with an air of apology, the choicest tidbits of lobster and dogfish in garlic sauce to tempt their old palates and a whole *oka* of *retzina* to replenish their glasses. There is nothing but gentleness and respect and deference in this, and yet the wine seems to be a libatory offering, the food a propitiation. And when Captain Miches or Mikailis or a great lusty diver offers the platter, his quietly spoken '*parakalo*' seems to take on more than its everyday meaning, 'please,' and become, what it is in its deeper sense — 'I pray.'

Sometimes, but not every night (for he is temperamental as a prima donna), old Georgios Makrinakis, the rag-doll man, can be persuaded to sing. He has only one song and, like himself, it is very old and very sad. It tells of the capture by the Turks of a gallant *Klepht*, a mountain guerrilla fighter. Georgios is, in fact, the last of the true Turkish ballad singers. He sings his song in the old manner, with the quavering throat and oddly inflected phrasing that is now a lost art. He has little voice left. The soaring, sustained throb of the climax '… he knows how to live with honour, and how to die he knows …' sometimes becomes a high-pitched nasal twangling, rather like the sort of noise we used to make as children by holding our noses and singing with the edges of our hands beating against our throats.

Yet it is not pity or kindness or amusement that makes the divers cajole and wheedle and plead with the old man to sing, nor is it politeness that holds them in a rigid silence until he flings his long, loose-jointed arm wide in a final tragic clown's gesture and rises on thin, shaking old man's legs to quaver the spine-chilling phrase, 'They have slain the Klepht!' The touch of genius is still there. It is only a touch now, but unmistakable through the scratches and cracks and weaknesses of a voice that is very old and was never trained. It is distorted and blurred, but clearly recognisable, as if one were listening to the young voice on an old wax recording. His sense of timing even now is faultless as Gielgud's.

No one else attempts to sing old Georgios' song, although one or two of the younger men imitate his manner. It is not the same, although Mikailis Mellekios, a Pan-faced shepherd from the mountains who often plays the *tsabuna* (a primitive Greek form of the bagpipes) in Skeftarios', converts it into a high, wild, abandoned keening that is not unlike the sound of the *tsabuna* itself. Another Mikailis, a dapperly dressed *ferneze* diver who always drinks with Fortes and Costas Manglis, sings the old style also, but it is his dancing that is notable. And when Mellekios the shepherd comes down from the mountains carrying his *tsabuna* tied up in a striped dishcloth there is always dancing, wild dancing, at Skeftarios'.

The *tsabuna* was made by Mikailis' grandfather. The sheepskin is as soft and flexible as old worn silk, and the olive-root horn is carved with stylised eagles and the same pattern of magic stars and circles that the daughters of George Vlamos, the potter, paint with white clay on the red Kalymnian water jars.

The *tsabuna* is a macabre object when inflated — a task, incidentally, for powerful lungs: I have seen the gigantic Captain

Miches fail in attempting it — a distended white trunk with a headless neck and two stumps of arms that end one in a pipe and the other in a horn. Dali's moustache would twitch with bliss at the spectacle of Mellekios cradling it lovingly.

It is pitched unearthly high, too high to be used effectively as an accompaniment to singing. Only Mellekios himself can sing to his own music but he, with his darting eyes, nut-brown face and sharp little white teeth seems scarcely human anyway. Twitch off his boots and you'll find hooves rapping out the rhythm, and there are certainly nubs of horns hidden in his coarse black tangled hair. He has a barefoot, nut-brown wife and five brown children who herd the sheep and the goats and dance in a ring on the mountains to their father's wild music. The third boy, Pantalés, is a little bit 'away' — a sorrowful, dumb child who clutches handfuls of air and weeps for I don't know what.

What is called 'Kalymnian' dancing is usually Cretan, with an occasional Lerian or Samian intrusion and one or two dances which are indigenous to the island. They are performed mostly by men, and the dancers, from five to ten in number, form a semicircle linked by hands. The leading dancer is separated from the next by a tautly held white handkerchief, which allows him the extra freedom of movement necessary to the development of his complicated improvisations — intricate steps, wild spins and leaps and the Cossack-like heel slappings which grow ever more audacious as the tempo develops. Only the leading dancer improvises. The second is a sort of pacemaker. He keeps the furious rhythm without ever departing from the precise set of formal steps. The third man follows the second, but the energy of the footwork diminishes with each dancer. The last man usually shuffles around the circle nonchalantly, exchanging badinage with the onlookers. When the leading dancer has completed half a dozen circles of improvisation he drops to the end of the line and the second dancer becomes the leader. The dance continues until every dancer has had the chance to demonstrate his skill in the leading role.

Half-way round the circle Sakialares, a gangling fifty-year-old diver with ears like handles, red-eyed and sodden from three months' solid drinking, weaves a maze of tiny, intricate steps. Only the speed of his footwork keeps him upright. He is three from the head of the line, but he has taken the leadership of the dance and whirled it to a point of frenzy. The *tsabuna* squeals, the brown fingers of Pan flicker across the horn of olive root. All the sea boots beneath the tables are thumping out the rhythm against the wooden floor.

'Come on, George!' Sakialares bellows suddenly, lurching from the circle to crash his great ham fist down on the table. Two glasses and a beaker of *retzina* go tumbling to the floor. He kicks the fragments of splintered glass beneath the table. 'Me all right, eh?' he bawls. 'You all right. These others — bah!' He glares belligerently around at the other tables. 'You — me — all right.' And he drags George from the table to join the dance. It is useless to protest or resist. Sakialares is as big as a house, and his hands are like plates. For two or three circles George stumbles good-naturedly at the end of the line, held in the grip of Sakialares as in a vice. Then he slowly begins to pick up the rhythm. Everyone in the *taverna* is helping him.

'*Ena! Ena-thio-trial! Ena! Ena-thio trial!*' At all the tables the men are clapping it out.

'You all right!' roars Sakialares delightedly, and his raised fist dares anyone to deny it. George, wearing an expression of happy concentration, points his toes and clicks his heels — '*Ena! Ena-thio-trial!*' — as all right as I've ever seen him.

'Sit down, Sakialares!' calls young Captain Charlie in some embarrassment. 'You're drunk!' Sakialares is an embarrassment to everyone. If he were not so greatly loved no *taverna* would have him. His nickname is *Seismos*, earthquake, and his capacity for destruction, catastrophe and mayhem is almost limitless.

'Drunk!' he bellows. 'You — me — all right George, eh? By-by we chuck up. All right!' He glowers towards the corner table. 'That Charlie he nothing. Charlie — *shit*!'

Young Captain Charlie blushes like a girl. It is almost the only English word that all of them know. Many of them who had contact with British or American or Australian soldiers in the war vaguely remember other words too — mostly of four letters, and all unsuitable for polite conversation. But they have forgotten their meanings and say the words to me seriously and politely, rather like children reciting a poem for which they expect to be applauded. They are speaking my tongue. It is their way of paying me a compliment, and I must smile and nod approvingly.

There is no vagueness, however, concerning the word that Sakialares has used. This has, by common usage, passed into their own dialect. By way of apology young Captain Charlie takes from his top pocket a tiny bottle of cheap Alexandrian scent and pours it over my hands. Charlie, who is the shyest and gentlest and quietest of the sponge captains, brings many bottles of scent back from his summer diving cruises to the Egyptian beds. With these bottles he is unfailingly gallant — to men as well as women. He is always known as 'young' Captain Charlie, although he is forty. He has not been married because no husband has yet been found for his sister, though her *prika* is enviable. Since she is, alas, long past her prime it would appear that Charlie is destined to permanent bachelorhood. Possibly here one can find an element of frustration responsible for the fact that Charlie, for all his shyness and quietness, is one of the port's most redoubtable gamblers, poker-faced, steely nerved and implacable. I have seen him lose ten thousand *drachmae* in an evening's play at a poker table without a flicker of expression on his face.

The old men in the corner are also discomfited by the word Sakialares has chosen, and old Nicko rolls across the room and presents me with three carnation heads. The giants nod their approval, and Captain Miches sends over a plate of *fooskas* by Golden Anna who on the way across the room absentmindedly forks up a couple of pieces of the black and crimson meat and chews on them ruminatively. Her husband, passing with a fistful of empty beakers, snorts to nobody in particular: 'That Anna, she eats like hell!'

The *tsabuna* wails higher and faster. Mellekios' sharp brown face is glistening with sweat. Under the table his boots stamp and leap as if his feet were dancing by themselves. No one but Mikailis the *ferneze* can keep such a pace. The circle disintegrates. Only one wildly spinning figure remains in the centre of the room.

Sakialares' drinking partner, a small, anonymous man in a cloth cap and a jersey intriguingly labelled *Westminster Fellowship* is, as usual, fast asleep. Sakialares picks him up and shakes him a little, tentatively, then drops him with a snort of disgust and weaves his way outside, no doubt to chuck up. Everybody breathes more easily. They are desperately anxious to assure me that Sakialares is a *poli kalo paithi*, a very good lad, when sober. He is a good husband, a good father, a fine diver. They vie with one another in tales of the generosity and charm, kindliness and goodness of Sakialares. It is the *krasi*, the wine, that makes him wild. For Sakialares there is a devil in the *krasi*.

Speaking of devils, asks Fortes suddenly, do I know how to put the devil in a bottle? Sakialares is forgotten in a sudden exchange of meaningful glances. It sounds like a lead into one of the schoolboyish pranks that the divers delight in, especially as Fortes is very drunk. But all the faces turned to me are quick with interest. Their eyes are earnest and sober. Obviously this is regarded as a perfectly serious question. I confess my ignorance.

All Kalymnian women know, says Costas Manglis darkly. There is a hasty movement of sunburnt hands sketching crosses. Golden Anna smiles enigmatically. I appeal to her as a reasonable woman. Her smile broadens and her grey bulk quivers with silent laughter. But she will not answer. Excepting only Mikailis Mellekios, all of the men look uncomfortable. Mellekios is cradling the deflated *tsabuna* and laughing too, with silently throbbing throat and sharp, twitching face.

Everything suddenly is very queer and baffling, and I am inclined to be cross and governessy and to demand rational explanations.

George is grinning. 'Go on,' he says. 'You're jealous. You can't have it *both* ways. You traded in devil bottling for trousers and a cigarette holder.'

There are enough grains of truth in this gibe to irritate me. But some old ineradicable knowledge lingers, like a worm burrowing silent secret tunnels in the validity of my sophisticated scorn and amusement.

If I stay long enough in Kalymnos it is not improbable that this old second memory might quicken. It is a fascinating and awesome prospect to consider. George will go to the *tavernas*. I won't have time. I'll be busy in the kitchen pantry with my sleeves rolled up, bottling devils like mad.

Kalymnian women do not go to *tavernas*. That my presence is never questioned probably is mostly due to the fact that I am a foreigner, and therefore beyond criticism, or else it is another example of the extreme sensitivity of the Greeks in the matter of hospitality. After the first still, shocked silence, when I sat among the barrels like Iphigenia among the Taurians, there was not a diver nor a captain who did not go to elaborate pains to welcome me and to make me feel at home. They would bring me rare shells wrapped in pieces of newspaper and great silky sponges from Alexandria and Benghazi. One night as we were going home from Skeftarios' with about a thousand *drachmae* worth of beautiful sponges clasped in our arms George said, 'One thing, if the novel is a flop we can always go into the sponge business. Or make shell jewellery and sell it to the passengers going down to Rhodes.'

Within a week or two, however, the careful politeness, formal and a little awkward, eased out into a genuine acceptance. I am sure it no longer occurs to any of them except old Georgios Makrinakis that I am trespassing on sacrosanct male ground. To the intense delight of George, the old ballad singer stubbornly clings to the accepted convention and refuses to regard me as being quite respectable; he winks at me dolefully with a sad blue eye or mournfully pinches my bottom as I pass. Not all the frantic whisperings of *Capitano* Anthonis nor the outraged indignation of Emmanuele Manglis are able to produce any change in his regretful roguishness. Equality of the sexes is too newfangled a notion for his poor old head to absorb.

It seems terribly unfair that the only other woman here who has dared brave the masculine stronghold of the *taverna* should be so severely criticised for it. But Mina is a Kalymnian born, and although she is the wife of an American citizen and has herself lived for many years in Athens, where women may drink in the *tavernas* as freely as men, she is subject to the same rules as her more downtrodden sisters. That she is the doting grandmother of three sturdy young Kalymnians appears only to worsen the case against her.

At forty-five Mina is not only very beautiful, she is also extremely chic. I have never seen her wear anything different from the black dress, striped apron and white coif that is the everyday working outfit of the island women, but her waist is like a girl's in spite of the six children she has borne, and she wears a coif as if Lili Dache had run it up for her in a moment of divine inspiration.

Nor is her presence condoned by the fact that her visits to the *tavernas* are specifically questing forays in search of her gregarious husband Tony, to tell him that supper is ready, that a man wishes to speak to him, that somebody has an *oka* of sponges to sell, that he will have a splitting headache in the morning if he has any more *retzina*. For she comes neither timidly, which is the proper attitude of a Kalymnian wife, nor shrewishly, which at least is an attitude the men understand, nor in a scolding frenzy, which is diverting. Mina comes with her eyes dancing, as if it is an enormous joke that she has to call Tony again, and she will always sit for a while and drink a glass or two of *retzina* and chat happily with everyone, for all the world as though she had a perfect right to be there.

Her husband Tony, a lovable extrovert, was by virtue of his English one of the first people we got to know well in Kalymnos. He is a happy man who has never ceased to thank God that he gave up his fairly lucrative cafe in Florida to return to the poverty of his dearly loved island. After Kalymnos his ruling passion is the English language (or, more correctly, those words of the English language that have more than three or four syllables), which, ironically, he uses to express his detestation of the English race, an inflammation rubbed raw by the Cyprian problem. He is a good man and one of the rare Greeks who brought back his soul intact from the trans-Atlantic crossing.

It was Tony who was basically responsible for the episode we have come to refer to as 'The Small Animus.' As it was not without its significance in reshaping certain aspects of Kalymnian life, the story is perhaps worth telling.

It was about New Year that the children, particularly Shane, who adds a special Florentine cunning to that natural capacity of the child for driving its elders to a point of desperation, began to become importunate.

'In London you *said* ... you *promised* ...'

'If children don't keep a promise they aren't true ... they're something *awful*. But grown-ups don't have to, do they, Mummy?' Shane's expression was about as guileless as that of a Borgia dining out with the House of Sforza.

That night George, conceding defeat, took up the matter with Tony. 'Listen, Tony,' he said anxiously, 'we've got to find some sort of pet for the children. When we were in London I promised they could have one. You know, some sort of —'

'Them kids!' Tony rose to his feet, raised his cloth cap and motioned for silence with the copper beaker. 'Mister George and Missus Charmian! When I confront certain elements ...'

This is his invariable opening for what is inevitably a long, tortuous and utterly incomprehensible harangue twisting its way to the final impassioned peroration on the iniquities of British rule in Cyprus. By the time he had reached this point we were two beakers of *retzina* ahead and slightly discouraged about everything, including Cyprus. The rest of the clientele of the big *taverna* of Tasos Zordos looked discouraged too, but then they couldn't follow even the single-syllable words. Tony sat down, flushed and puffing a little with the pride of accomplishment.

'That's fine, Tony,' George said warily. 'Now, about the children, and that —'

'The children?' Tony studied him blankly. 'What have the children got to do with — with ... What is that goddam word now? Just now I *used* it! With ... Kids ain't concerned with —

with *imperialism*!' He beamed. 'That's it! Imperialism! You know, Mister George, when I confront certain elements —'

'Yes, Tony, that's fine. But the children want a pet. A small animal of some sort.'

'A small animus!' He shook his head hopelessly, his eyes dazed. 'Kids is crazy elements,' he said wonderingly. 'Why do they go around wanting *that* for? Ain't they got this climate? Ain't they got a panorama Rockefeller couldn't buy?'

'An animal, Tony. A small animal. You know how children are … a little dog, or a little cat of their own to look after … some sort of animal.'

Comprehension lighted his plump face with the mysterious joy of a child listening to a seashell.

'Ah, a small animus! Woof-woof-woof! Miaow-miaow!' He slapped his thigh delightedly and again banged for silence. 'Listen here, you fellers, all of you. Petros, Anastasis, Dimitri, Leonidas, Mikailis, listen you now. The children require the animus, creatures that are small and alive. You fetch them now.

'Tomorrow you bring them to the house of our friends. You understand what I mean? Small ones.'

'Only one, Tony,' George said urgently. 'One will do beautifully.'

'Poof?' said Tony. 'These fellers bring you plenty. Don't you worry no more now.' He shook his head admiringly. 'Them kids of yours is the craziest element. Why,' he said, 'this town is full of animus!'

'Yes,' George said bleakly, suddenly grey with the realisation of what we had done. 'I know.'

They began to come at dawn, when the mountains were washed rose pink and the zigzag trail to Vathy looked like a decorative motif scrawled across them. The cubes of the houses were dark, just a faint shelly gleam to them. From the window we could see the *Andros* at anchor out beyond the sponge boats, lighted up in the darkness like Selfridge's at Christmas.

The children were awakened by the first thuds on the street door, and before we could stop them they were hurtling down the stairs. By the time we had scrambled out and fumbled for candle and matches they had drawn the bolt and were squealing upstairs again, towing behind them a polite and grinning young sponge diver who rather sheepishly produced from his pocket a scraggy, bulging-eyed black kitten. It hung in his bleeding hand for a second before it bounded to the floor and scuttled into the kitchen with Martin and Shane in rapturous pursuit.

'Well,' said George, after we had thanked the young man and bathed his wounds in Dettol, 'at least it wasn't a donkey. Or a goat.'

'You wait,' I said. Down beneath the dark salt trees I could just make out the lean shape of Manolis. He was walking very carefully and holding well away from his body a large and heaving sack. Behind him, skipping around the tree boles, was Vassilis the cigarette boy, and there was certainly something else on his wooden tray besides cigarettes. Something that wriggled.

'*Mum!*' Martin wailed from the kitchen. 'The kitten's up the chimney. And it's all *oily!*' Suppressed giggles from Shane, pattering back in her pyjamas. 'I think it's *done something* in the oilcan.'

'Never mind about that,' George said shortly. 'Just you get downstairs as fast as you can and bolt that door again.'

Too late. It was nearly midday before we got the door bolted again, and by that time it seemed that half the inhabitants of the town had come and gone, albeit with some bewilderment, having made their small presentations. They had come singly and in groups of two or three, the tall men with the fierce black moustaches and shy brown eyes. They had come with sacks and bulging pockets and baskets covered with clean checked cloths. George was ashen. Even the frenzied rapture of the children had staled. They walked warily, with their mouths open like cretins.

Apart from the kitten up the chimney — where it stayed for a whole day, until smoked out — there were seven others, hissing and spitting from every dark corner and beneath all the beds. Not Listen-with-Mother kittens either. These were the torn-eared, raw-boned, fanged and clawed children of their alley parents, and they weren't having any truck with friendly advances.

On the balcony a fierce, red-eyed duck stomped backward and forward, hurling imprecations at the interested crowd assembled at the waterfront below. And in the kitchen Sevasti clucked away in disapproving counterpoint to the despairing clucking of the trussed red hen lurching around the stone floor. Under George's table two mangy little dogs shivered in cowed company, terrified, no doubt, of the swoops and sickening thuds of the three panic-stricken sparrows that just would not fly out of the open window. In the centre of it all a very small white rabbit with long black ears sat imperturbably in a soup plate, munching a cabbage leaf.

There was something awfully charming about that little rabbit. If the other spitting, clawing, furred and feathered monsters were straight from Bosch, the rabbit was the purest Disney.

Even at the awful climax of the nightmare, when George was hauling cats and dogs out from beneath the beds and the children were shrieking woe and Sevasti was grimly slaughtering the duck and the hen in the kitchen, the rabbit retained its composure, its boulevard air of *savoir-faire*. It seemed to possess some inner certainty that it would survive the debacle and could afford to devote its attention to the delicate task of pulling away the outer leaves of the cabbage to reach the succulent heart.

'That all them fellers brought you — just that one small animus?' Tony asked that night. Expertly he picked up the little rabbit by the ears and jiggled it around a bit. A long string of lettuce hung from its front teeth, and even dangling in mid-air it kept ascending and disappearing at the same steady rate. 'He's O.K.,' Tony said judicially. 'You keep him a bit, feed him up nice, he'll make a kilo maybe. A little butter, a few onions ...'

We had no intention of eating him, I said in what was meant to be a firm voice but was still rather a subdued tone because of the day's events. He was to be the children's pet.

He was a nice little pet too. I had never had any particular feeling about rabbits before. Australians are not normally reared in the Flopsy Bunny tradition. Rabbits were a pest, a vermin or a quarry for hunters. And it was as hunters that my brother and sister and I had wandered over the brown hills on dusky Saturday evenings, following my father and the big old-fashioned twelve-bore double-barrelled shotgun. Later my brother had a gun too, a Winchester .22, which sometimes I was allowed to use. The dead rabbits were very soft and heavy, and we used to slit one of the back legs, push the other through the slit and thread the carcasses on a long stick to carry home. Our family was poor and the meat welcome. We nearly always had baked or casseroled rabbit for Sunday dinner. 'Underground mutton,' my father would say. My later years in England did nothing to change my attitude. At bedtime I would read the children the Beatrix Potter books, but I never could get worked up about myxomatosis.

The bright-eyed little character in the soup bowl, however, seemed to have no connection with those long-ago Saturday slaughters among the brown grasses and prickly lantana, or with the diseased carcasses strewn across the Cornish kale fields. He was pretty and Disneyesque, and he appeared, besides, to possess a degree of intelligence quite remarkable in a rabbit. That is to say, he would come when called, sit up and beg and suffer himself to be lugged around in the streets by the children without protest. One way and another we lavished quite a lot of affection on him, and on the whole he responded about as well as a rabbit can. We never did succeed in house-training him, but perhaps this was not so much perverseness on his part as an overestimation of his intelligence on ours. This and a tiresome habit of chewing the legs of chairs were all Sevasti had against him. She would mutter a little as she swept rattling showers of pellets down the stairs, but she would also bring bundles of fresh, juicy grasses every other day.

'Eeeh! He's making good meat now!' she would say to us admiringly. Calliope from the corner shop would come puffing up the stairs twice a week, her greasy apron filled with radish tops and cabbage leaves. 'To make sweet flesh,' she would hiss knowledgeably.

Mikailis scoured the rocky hilltops above Saint Vassilias for milk thistles and brought them down in the white cloth the labourers use to pad their shoulders under the heavy dragrope of the carts. The rabbit accepted all these offerings equally, and in a short time became huge and lethargic, preferring now to spend his days sprawled languorously beneath the desk. 'If you don't eat him soon he won't taste so good,' warned Yanni anxiously. 'Old rabbits get a funny taste — rank.'

This was exactly the sort of talk which for weeks had terrified the children, to the point that whenever Sevasti or Yanni appeared they would snatch up the Animus and dive for the street, where they would hide him down drainpipes or among the flour sacks on a stationary *karro*. There was even one occasion when we found him concealed among the peanuts in the basket of Dimitri, the *fistikia* boy. The rabbit appeared to take no harm from these adventures, nor even to become nervous, as another rabbit might.

I told Yanni that I would as soon consider eating one of the children. The enormity of this remark caused him to treat me warily for quite some time. I suspect that he spat three times whenever he entered the house.

After all the drama latent in the threat of knives, the end of the Animus was rather silly. He crawled through a gap in the balcony railing one morning (I cannot imagine what possessed him to stir himself to such an energetic feat!), fell into the *plateia* and broke his neck.

The grief of the children — racked by a passion of love and loss beyond their comprehension — was insupportable.

'There, there,' Sevasti crooned unhappily, desperate to find some means of consolation. 'I will make a beautiful soup of your little rabbit. Georgios will go now to milk the ewe, and Georgia will bring fresh onions —' The violence of the terror and revulsion caused by this offer nearly frightened Sevasti out of her wits. I found her in the kitchen with a face as white as the children's, dashing cold water over the bedraggled black head of the Animus.

'Blessed Mother of God, send us a miracle!' she prayed passionately.

The news spread like wildfire. On the dangling heels of the Animus, as it were, came fat Calliope with a bunch of spring onions, Mikailis, whose regular supplies of milk thistles gave him the right to advise on culinary procedure and Yanni, full of congratulations on this fortuitous solution to our moral scruples, bearing a carafe of *retzina* to accompany the feast. The grief of the children quickly transformed their festive interest into a dismayed bewilderment. Greeks love children dearly, and are quick to recognise tragedy when they see it.

'*Po-po-po-po!*' Mikailis muttered uncomfortably. 'I never meant that you should eat the rabbit, my darlings. I will take it away. You need never know *who* eats it.'

'I will take it, nephew,' muttered Calliope hoarsely. 'Irini does well enough at beans, but a rabbit now … A rabbit needs a *cook* to get the best out of him. Besides, have I not fed this animal on the best, the tenderest radish leaves? If those thistles of yours,' she glared, 'have not soured his flesh, he will be —'

'Fools!' Sevasti was crouched over the sodden bundle of fur like a tigress defending her young. Her eyes blazed. 'Nobody will eat this animal. It is not the English custom. Can't you see that the children suffer? One of you must take it and put it in the *thalassa*.'

'The fish will eat it,' said Mikailis simply.

Yanni, who had been vainly trying to establish contact with the two shocked and offended children, now put down the *retzina* carafe with an air of renunciation.

'There is only one thing to do,' he said solemnly. 'We must bury this animal.'

Calliope looked as if she would explode, but for the first time since the discussion began the children turned great, swollen, considering eyes on the assembled company.

'Do you mean … *properly*?' Martin's voice was a queer croak. He had reached the stage of hiccoughs.

'Oh, properly!' Yanni promised recklessly.

Shane wiped the back of her fist across her nose, choked on a sob and said, 'With a coffin and remembrances and *everything*?'

Yanni gulped slightly. 'Everything,' he said staunchly. 'That is, if *Theia* Calliope has a box that is the proper size.'

Theia Calliope glowered at her nephew, her throat mottled and red and working like a turkey's. But she was bereft of speech.

Sevasti said menacingly that she was quite sure *Kyria* Calliope had a box of exactly the right size. They would go together and fetch it immediately. As they went down the stairs she was whispering urgently in Calliope's ear.

'Since this is Greece,' said Martin pedantically, 'it will have to be an Orthodox funeral, won't it, Dad?'

His face was blotched with tears, but his eyes were shining.

'It will,' said George.

The rabbit was buried gloriously at dusk, in a cardboard box scattered with jonquils and daisies and the minute tin and plastic crosses collected by the children from innumerable christening parties and Shane's remembrances. George and I had by this time begun to feel a little silly and very much embarrassed, particularly as an earlier attempt by the children to bury their pet themselves had been thwarted by a band of nearly a hundred Kalymnian children who had raided the burial party half-way up the mountain and routed it in their eagerness to participate in the funeral. However, the coffin and body had been safely brought back to the house, albeit a little battered, and to mollify the children in this second disaster we had rashly agreed to be present at the evening cortège. Our fear of committing a sacrilege and of gravely offending the religious sensibilities of the people we hoped to overcome by sneaking the box under George's jacket and strolling up the mountainside in a casual manner, as if we were taking an evening walk.

It was obvious from the large and grave assembly at our door that such a subterfuge was no longer possible. The word had spread that the Australians were observing a curious national custom. The town had turned out respectfully to honour us.

Solemnly we turned down the alley where the wide concrete stairway ascends to the upper levels of the town. Solemnly the procession followed us. The children, either overcome by the dignity of the occasion or, perhaps feeling that it was expected of them, began to weep again, snuffling away damply in the warm, thick dust.

Women leaned in the yellow lamplighted squares of doors and windows, or squatted in the cobbled streets beside their charcoal tins, stirring supper pots. All the alley smelled of beans stewing in olive oil.

'What is happening?' they called as we passed. Hastily adjusting headscarves and aprons, they left their cooking pots to run after us. By the time we reached the top of the stairs the procession was fifty strong, and all across the mountain slope dark figures were flitting among the scattered houses, converging on us. The children clustered close about Martin and Shane suddenly began to chant softly. Behind us a woman took up the chant and tossed it, shrill and unexpected, down the massed moving line.

The ludicrous reason for the procession was lost and forgotten. We were caught in something else, an old rite the meaning of which had melted in a time lost long ago but the form of which was part of that dim race memory we inherit at our births. That wild cry of lamentation was not for a stiffening rabbit. It was for Tammuz dead, or the springing red flowers where Adonis' blood was scattered, or a woodland king torn on the sacrificial oak. Straining and stumbling on the loose boulders we toiled up the dusk-wreathed mountain. The chanting rose deep and sad from a hundred throats, and a boy with a torch (or a lantern or a candle or a blazing cypress brand) moved to the head of the line and led us on. High over the noble rock that soars above the town one star hung in the great blue night. I thought perhaps we were climbing to reach it.

We buried the rabbit under some stones half-way up the donkey trail that leads to Agios Petros. It was now quite dark, and we had climbed nearly to the top of the mountain. Everyone seemed rather dazed and confused. The boy with the torch shone the beam on the rocks for us, and there was a note of hysteria in his high, excited laugh as we hurriedly covered the Animus over. Shane set the box of remembrances beside it, and everyone began to giggle and shout. We all trooped down the mountainside in a mood of high hilarity. Only *Theia* Calliope stayed behind, carefully arranging a little cairn of rocks.

'That's so she'll know where to dig it up later,' George said. 'For stew.'

That was all there was to it. In the morning Yanni brought another little black and white rabbit and spent all day making a slatted hutch with a hinged door and a rain-proof roof. And the next day Calliope came again with *radichi*, and Sevasti with fresh grass, and Mikailis with milk thistles.

Although we kept that rabbit for a long time we somehow never developed for it the affection we had had for the first *kouneli*. The children began to harbour more ambitious thoughts about puppies and donkeys. Yanni, on the other hand, seemed to love the creature passionately, even when it grew into a sort of gaunt, loping Gary Cooper of a rabbit with ears that seemed comically long even for one of his species. Sevasti, too, would pet it for hours and never once complained of the litter of pellets that had to be swept up each day. For months Calliope and Mikailis continued to supply fresh food with a methodical solicitude their own children never knew. There was never any mention of knives or cooking pots.

At Easter the spring grasses were cut to feed the Pascal lambs which every family had bought for the Easter Sunday feasts. By the end of April the hills were brown and parched, and it had become a daily chore to find food to satisfy the rabbit's gargantuan appetite. Mikailis reported worriedly that there were no milk thistles on the mountain. Sevasti would rise at dawn to scour the hillsides, but some days she would find nothing and others only a few dry brown stalks. The *radichi* had disappeared from the market, and lettuces were costly.

'We'll have to get rid of it,' George said finally and, in some relief, I agreed. The children, utterly indifferent to its fate, said they would give it away to someone.

After wandering about with the huge animal — all of two kilos now, and in the pink of condition — they returned at lunchtime with the creature still in their arms. Nobody, they said in some perplexity, would take it. 'All the mothers said they couldn't afford to buy the proper food for it,' Martin explained.

'Well, for heaven's sake, they could eat —' I stopped abruptly, realising what I had almost said.

'Oh, I told them what lovely soup it would make,' Shane said callously. 'It was funny, Mummy. All the ladies crossed themselves and spat three times.'

Yanni, white-faced but determined, for the first time openly criticised us. We ought to be ashamed of ourselves, he said. The rabbit, he said accusingly, knew no father or mother but us. It was, he added with dignity, like Tarzan growing up with the orang-utans, believing they were his own kind.

Sevasti turned her head away, performed her household duties with compressed lips and expressed her displeasure by never once speaking to us directly all day. The rabbit, guided perhaps by instinct to where loyalty lay, loped about at her heels, and every now and then she would pick it up and stroke its grotesque ears sadly.

Finally American Mike, the most materialistic of our friends, was persuaded to take it. By this time I had come actively to dislike the animal. If I could have found someone to kill it for me I would have stewed it with sadistic pleasure and picked the bones clean.

'Well,' I said brightly, a few days later, 'how did the rabbit taste?'

American Mike pushed the cap to the back of his head and scratched his wiry hair. He looked rather sheepish. 'Well, to tell the truth, Mister Charmian, we didn't get round to eating it after all. Fotini took on so, and that girl Maria of mine. Jesus Christ, Mister Charmian! *Women!* They said it would bring bad luck and I might as well go and drown myself now as kill that rabbit and then go off sponging to Africa. Funny,' he said thoughtfully, 'I never did hear that before. Not about a goddam rabbit. It's something new they got into their heads.'

'Well, what's happened to the rabbit?'

'Oh, it's still around the house,' he said. 'Fotini keeps feeding it leaves off the grapevine. I guess there'll be enough to last until there's some grass or something about again.'

10

Under the bright blue and yellow map of Greece, which is stuck to the wall with scraps of adhesive plaster, the midday meal is set out on the table. Books and typing paper, carbons and letter files have been pushed back against the wall to make room for the plates. The big map is still holding to the wall, although the wind has turned to the north — the *boreas*, the dry wind that always curls the adhesive off and tumbles the map face downwards across the dishes.

On the table are firm pink tomatoes that came in big baskets in the morning caique from Vathy, a dish of pale shining cucumbers, cold *smarithes*, tan coloured and crunchy, a loaf of new brown bread pricked with sesame seed, a round white Kalymnian cheese still smelling of the herbs it was wrapped in, dark thin honey from the whitewashed hives at Argos and the first of the sweet, heavy melons that will be piled on every stall in the market all the summer through. The melon has been cooled overnight and through the morning within the wet hessian walls of the coolsafe that stands for the summer in the draught between the window overlooking the cool green harbour waters and another overlooking the still, hot *plateia*, prematurely abandoned to siesta.

Martin is seated already. His bruised brown legs are twined blissfully beneath the chair, his cropped corn-stubble head lowered absorbedly as he peels transparent curls of skin from his nose and cheekbones. All over his dark face are irregular pink patches.

George is hacking thick chunks of bread with the Astypalian knife, a lovely thing with a horn handle studded with coloured discs of bone. This was the gift of a fisherman at Vathy.

Shane, inevitably, is missing. '*Pou ine* Shane? — Where is Shane?' has become almost a family catch cry.

'She came back from swimming half an hour ago,' George says. 'She was in the kitchen feeding Nike and Heleni with tomatoes. I imagine Sevasti chased them all out.'

'They were on Dimitri's caique playing five-stones, or something,' Martin submits disinterestedly. 'A sailor chased them off. When he went away they all climbed back on again.' He takes a thin shred of skin between his fingers and scrutinises it intently.

Dimitri's caique is moored just around the corner in front of the engineering shop. Nike and Heleni, apparently having tired of five-stones, are taking turns crawling up and down the thin, splintered plank that rests precariously against the high, faded stern of the boat. The feat is made more difficult by the fact that each of them is clutching a thick slab of bread spread with olive oil and sugar, which I presume is their lunch.

'Nike! Heleni!' I call softly from the shore so that I do not disturb their balance. The water is not very deep and the two of them can swim, but Heleni is wearing the overlarge and rather faded cotton dress that came in the parcel from America, and she is terribly proud of it. She is an eager, undersized little girl, with damp, tilted eyes and two very large front teeth which, like the new dress, she hasn't grown into yet. Nike has no relatives in America, so she wears what looks like one of her father's shirts, hacked off at the bottom and sleeves. Her coarse, matted hair is hacked as ruthlessly as the shirt. If only someone cared about her a bit she might lose that aggressive truculence which in the early days had caused my children to label her the Kicker.

'*Pou ine* Shane?' Nike skitters down the wobbling plank to tell me that Shane went to the beach with *Theia* Calliope, who was taking her ewe to be washed in the sea.

The hot half-moon of grey pebbles behind the Italian-built customs house is littered with children, spread wet and dark and shining on the hot stones like starfish, oblivious of the pangs of hunger or the allure of siesta. Down by the summer café of wooden poles roofed with dried branches of oleander a few young men still sprawl inertly in splendid male isolation. At a decent distance beyond them, on the rocks that fringe the thin pier running out to the lighthouse, half a dozen women sit with their skirts tucked up and their beating paddles laid aside, waiting for the spread rugs of crimson and black and grey and yellow to dry before folding them and taking them home to store away, warm and smelling of the sea and sunshine, for the summer.

A gang of men from the Lavassi shipyard are burning the paint from the hull of a very old high-powered caique beached well above the slope of shingle. It was dragged out of the water yesterday, hauled laboriously from the shallows across flat balks of timber greased with pig fat, with forty men and lads trudging around two primitive capstans. It had come ashore almost imperceptibly, a fraction of an inch at a time, but now it was high on the beach, and the men had lit great fires of gorse beneath the bilge. They were standing well back from the blackening hull, still holding aloft the blazing brands of orange flame. Indifferent to the drama of the conflagration, unaware of the visible implications of this working system three thousand years older than the blowtorch, regardless of the beauty of the tense, half-naked men gleaming palely against the leaping flames and the soaring charcoal curve of the old ship, *Theia* Calliope was wallowing fully clothed in the shallows with the tightly ringleted ewe cuddled firmly into her lap.

'*Cherete, Kyria* Calliope!'

'Ah, *cherete, Kyria!*' She beams and sloshes water over the head of the sheep. 'Come in and join us.'

'I can't. I'm looking for Shane. Her lunch is ready. Was she with you?'

'Indeed she was. She played in the water with the ewe for a long time, but then she ran away. I don't know where.'

'Mike Mellekios was herding goats down to the slaughterhouse,' one of the men with the torches yelled. 'That's where she went.'

The road to the slaughterhouse follows the sea. It is a narrow, rubbled track of many steps and levels, pitted with holes and littered with boulders of various sizes that have remained there since the plan to construct a motor road to the *therma* was abandoned. (The *therma* is reputed to be one of Greece's finest medicinal hot springs. The Italians built a concrete pavilion over the waters, with baths inside, but like every other public building in Kalymnos it has now fallen into disrepair. One would need to be miserably afflicted or to have great faith in the healing properties of the waters to brave the stench that hangs about the fallen roof and unhinged door and slimy tanks like an almost visible aura!) The slaughterhouse is the last building before the unfinished road swings around the shoulder of a big cliff, and to reach it you pass through the area most badly hit during the British bombing of the island. The cubes of houses straggling up the steep, rocky mountain slope are mostly only roofless shells. Inside them weeds grow rankly through the accumulated household rubbish of a decade. By day the ragged children play there. At night goats and sheep huddle on the collapsed bedshelves or in the crumbling kitchen alcoves, and hens and turkeys roost along the fallen rafters. Perhaps one house in four remains habitable. As one might expect, these are occupied almost invariably by sponge divers and their families.

The combination of poverty, desuetude, litter and devastation should make this a squalid area, but the occupied houses are so clean and brightly painted, the rugs that hang among the debris and ruins so vividly coloured, the animals and children so vigorous and healthy, the air so heady with the smell of salt and sunshine and herbs, that the ruins take on the look of a stage set, brilliantly lit by the great burning noonday sun. Looking down from the road at the turquoise sea and purple rocks glimpsed through broken walls, hanging window-frames and the serene apricot arches of an old Turkish house, one cannot resist the feeling that the wild fig growing through the pink wall, the grey paintless rail hanging from a long-abandoned bed, the yellow-eyed goat standing heraldic on a fallen pediment have all been carefully arranged for one's aesthetic appreciation. In the hot and shadowless midday all is revealed. One looks through doors and windows at a floor of weeds where four children squat bare-bottomed behind boulders among the shards of old water jars and cooking pots, and a second later sees through what seem to be identical windows a woman and children grouped on a bare board floor about a big earthen bowl of tomatoes and cucumbers set out on a low round table covered with a clean checked cloth. It is hard to find the line between habitation and desolation. The whole area is *occupied*. The sun lights it all, indiscriminately, and the same smell of animals, children, olive oil, sea salt and defecation pervades every stone and crevice.

The slaughterhouse is at some distance from the last of the habitations and at a lower level. You can smell the hot, strong smell of blood long before you reach it — the sea is stained dark and dreadful for fifty yards out — and some young boys down on the rocks are carefully rinsing bladders and intestines. Three wooden mule carts are being loaded with carcasses that still trickle slow streams of scarlet. Beside a concrete slab the municipal doctor examines the hearts and lights and livers and kidneys of the slaughtered beasts. A clerk beside him with a rubber stamp slaps purple imprints on the still-warm skins of those animals that have passed the medical inspection.

Beside the mules Mikailis Mellekios stands draped in the red and slippery skins of six small goats. He is behind a fawn-coloured mule, and I have the curious illusion that the shaggy legs and hooves of the animal are his. With his Pan face and crimson forearms and the bloody hides around his shoulders he is a Centaur come from some ancient sacrificial rite.

'*Ee-eeeeh, Kyria!*' he calls in his high, sharp shepherd's voice. 'Come and see the fine skins I have. That shepherd's bag you wanted … come, look at these!'

The blood on his arms, on his boots, on the dangling skins, has a ruby gleam. The colour is solidified and polished. It will be hard and crystalline to the touch, not wet at all — yet the drops are still falling slowly, one by one, into the dust near the cloven feet. I excuse myself hastily and politely. I have not the time today. Has he seen Shane?

'Ah, the *koritzaiki*? She came along with me, happy as a kid on the mountain. I sat her up high so no blood spurted on her when we did the killing. She started to cry when we began skinning them. Apostoli called that *yieneka* of Miches' and she took her off somewhere.'

I pelt back along the road now to the house of Miches, whom we know better as American Mike. Mike is away now on one of the sponge boats off Benghazi, but we keep contact through the occasional letters he sends to his wife Fotini. Fotini, a plain, pleasant woman of middle age, is on the balcony under the grapevine, spinning a long thin strand of wool from the teased fawn tufts held in a forked stick stripped smooth of its bark. When the wool has been spun and twisted and washed in the sea it will no doubt be knitted into socks or vests or a new jersey for Mike.

'Kalós!' Fotini smiles, bending forward to kiss me. 'You're looking for Shane?' Like all Kalymnians, who have never encountered such a name before, she pronounces it 'Say.' It is always 'O Martis and Say.'

Breathlessly and with a lingering sense of horror I say that I am.

'Ah, sit down a minute and rest. The *koritzaiki* is all right.' As if there is all the time in the world (and for a woman who every year must wait seven months before her husband comes home, I suppose there is) she puts down the forked stick and the spindle and unhurriedly prises open the lid of the cistern. The bucket clangs and shakes down on its rope with that hollow thud and gurgle that is the music of a well, and she hauls it up again filled with sweet cold water, which she offers me in a clean glass exactly centred on a blue-bordered plate. '*Si-yia-sas*,' she says politely and refills my empty glass and brings a plate of dried figs to place on the *sterna* beside me. Then she resumes her spinning.

'Was she very upset?' I ask anxiously. In spite of the well water and the wholesome smell of cleanliness surrounding Fotini's house, the smell of blood lingers in my nostrils.

Fotini peers at me wonderingly from beneath the folds of her headscarf. 'Upset? She was crying a little, that's all. All children cry. That's nothing. I gave her bread and oil and some figs, and Maria took her up to see Xanthippe's new baby.'

By the side of the ugly big church of Agios Nikolas a steep and narrow flight of stairs cleaves crookedly up for a hundred yards through the clustered houses and ends abruptly below the higher levels, so that if you want to visit *epano* you must scramble over the boulders and worm your way through people's houses as best you can. Fortunately Xanthippe's house is only half-way up, a rough blue-washed oblong rising from the dazzling blue-washed stairs, its aubergine shutters closed now against the sun.

Inside it is dark and stifling. Only the few plates in the wooden plate rail glimmer a cold bone white. On the raised bedshelf is a pale, sheeted mound that I rightly assume to be Xanthippe, who dozes beneath four gaudy framed prints of the adventures of Genovefa and innumerable cheap paper *ikons*. In the corner of the shelf old Anna the midwife squats with her eyes closed, her tufted chin slackly hanging among the loosened folds of her scarf, one hand loosely holding the string of the diminutive hammock. The hammock rocks almost imperceptibly against a large and unrecognisable photograph of Xanthippe with a bright-red mouth and bright-blue eyes which stare out with wild disbelief from beneath a crumpled *frou* of white net. The tiny hammock is covered with little crosses and charms and beads and bells. I assume that it must be a boy at last.

Xanthippe's four daughters are scattered across the floor like abandoned dolls. One clutches in her curled fist a half-chewed cucumber, at which a black hen is pecking desultorily. Three new kittens that look exactly like little black mice make squirming, soundless pleas from an upturned basket of potatoes. I shoo the hen out of the door and follow it quietly.

In the strange, still world of hot noontime I no longer care very much where my own child is. All life is retreating indoors. The mule carts carrying tomorrow's meat are far down the empty *plateia*, almost at the market, moving slowly in a small jingle of bells. The burning grey beach is deserted, and the sea is still. Even the flames that cradled the black ship have become soft ash. Below me, in the asphalted courtyard of Agios Nikolas, four labourers sleep in a blue wedge of shade, their folded white cloths tucked beneath their heads. Brilliant against the dazzling stairs a barefooted woman climbs slowly up from the sea, her head erect under a pile of black and crimson rugs.

A rough pathway runs along the top of the high retaining wall that makes a fortress of the upper levels. Without lifting my eyes I can look directly at the gilded cross surmounting the green dome of Agios Nikolas. High above the cobbled twists of empty streets, above the sleeping harbour and the ships, I move alone and silent in a white effulgence of light. The sound of chanting that wells up the wide ascending stair seems inevitable, a vocal utterance of worship to the source of this pure incandescence that is pouring down on the world — *Be still and know that I am God!* The fringed brazen standards, the spindly black-ribboned cross are molten gold, drawn to the source of light, defying gravity, flowing up the cracked concrete steps.

Two chanting priests wearing white copes over their black robes climb heavily upward, their bearded faces trickling with sweat. Around them the small ragged boys who carry the cross and the banners try to slow their own effortless pace and to compose into becoming gravity their grinning, self-important faces.

At the top of the stair I wait while they pass. The priests' beards are damply curled on their chins like the beards of Assyrians. Their open, chanting mouths are wet and pink. From their shabby robes comes a hot, fusty smell of old cloth and sweat. The buns of hair twisted on the backs of their necks have a shiny grey look, like peeled onions. The knot of people who follow them — a dozen women dressed in black, four bare-headed men bowed beneath an open coffin of plain wood — seem stupefied by heat.

It is a very old man in the coffin, swaddled and swathed and bandaged like Xanthippe's new baby in the little hammock. As the coffin passes I look down at the jutting crag of the nose, the long stubbled chin, the hands strapped firmly with a torn strip of lace into a position of pious resignation.

119

'He wouldn't have kept,' one of the women hisses to me as she passes, 'another *minute!*'

The coffin bumps the cornerstone and the corpse appears to stir slightly, as if about to remonstrate with the woman. Then it grates against the wall and lurches past. Behind it comes a thickset man bearing the coffin lid of new wood, held vertically to display the cross. Not until the lid had swayed past me do I observe the small, intent figure pattering along behind it — the small figure in the dirty sundress, yellow hair hanging in lank, sweaty strands on bare, salt-caked shoulders, tears and grime and salt crusted on her cheeks, her mouth set into a firm, determined line that is only slightly blurred by the granules of sugar stuck in the oil with which it is smeared. One hand holds the gathered folds of her skirt, which is bulging curiously. The other is held in the claw-like grip of a very old but extremely spry *gorgona*.

She is still protesting bitterly and vociferously as we turn out of the alley into the *plateia*.

'I *had* my lunch. I *had*! *I had!* One lady gave me figs in her house, and another who had a new baby gave me tomatoes and I had bread and oil with sugar with Themolena and Calliope and two *caramellos* from the man who was killing the goats.'

High on the parched brown mountainside the sun catches fire on the bronze standards. The toiling little procession has reached the blue gates of Agios Vassilias.

'What have you got in your skirt, my Polly?' George heaves her effortlessly up the stairs.

'What is it, Shaney? *What?*' Martin looks up interestedly from where he is sprawled on the floor with Apostoli and Georgouli, sorting shells.

A slow, radiant smile spreads over Shane's filthy little face. Very slowly she opens out the folds of her skirt, 'Look!' she says.

On top of a squelchy mass of squashed tomatoes and dried figs a tiny orange kitten is spreadeagled with its toothpick legs stretched out horizontally from a body as big as a sparrow. Its eyes are glued shut, its mouth is plaintively opening and shutting over teeth like needles.

'The lady with the baby gave it to me. It's just born out of its mother like the lady's little baby.'

'But, *sweetheart*! You'll have to take it back to its mother for a little while. It's too small.'

'But she *gave* it to me. She *did*!'

'But, darling, it can't eat yet. You wouldn't want the little kitten to die, would you?'

The blue eyes of both children turn slowly to each other in a long, speculative glance that has a new and fiendish gleam to it.

High on the mountainside the bells of Agios Vassilias begin to toll, three slow chimes and a pause, and three again ...

II

'The winter is soon past here,' Manolis had said. The last drops of rain fell on the first of April and there was not another shower, nor even a cloud in the sky, until November. But winter had been over long before April. It lasted for less than two months. Yet those two months were so crammed with tensions, terrors, high excitements, aching miseries, dreams and discoveries that our first Kalymnian winter seems to have a quite separate compartment in my memory, divorced from what had led up to it and what was to follow from it. It has somehow come to be, as it were, a slice of time complete in itself, a solid block of vivid experience that cannot be notched off into weeks and days and hours, that cannot even be truly related to the life we live here now.

It is a series of sharp, dramatic pictures fused together with lightning, thunderbolts, tempestuous seas, storms that split the heavens open, wild singing, drunken revels. I know that there were sunny days, but my memory is filled with torrents sweeping the boulders down the hills and mountains streaming sulphurous clouds. I know that we worked very hard, but in my memory we are eating and drinking and singing and dancing wildly in lamplit blue rooms among crowding dark faces. A muddy torrent pours across the *plateia*, bringing down the yellow earth and the rocks from the high levels. The children are wading in it with frills of dirty foam at their knees. There is a slaty wave crashing over the war memorial, and a dead pig, swollen by the sea, washes against the door of George Boulafendi's coffee-house. Men in slickers are dragging chains and anchors through the streets, leaning on the wind. Against our window masts toss crazily. Martin is running through a hailstorm, his mouth open, shouting to us, but there is no sound save the drumming of ice pellets. We are crawling around the corners of buildings, clinging to window-frames and doors, and beneath us the cobbled street is part of the fuming sea. In my memory everything is elemental, furious, beyond the edge of normality and control. I have pictures of men in black caps, roaring up the mountain to orange doors that open on crowded rooms embellished with Swiss oleographs of lakes and châteaux … soft, shawled women circling in spinning rooms … Martin and Shane holding long candles beside a great brass bowl, and an old white-bearded priest with his sleeves rolled up, holding high a naked, screaming baby dripping with oil and wine. All the tastes are still strange and marvellous on my tongue. The very food we ate then, the wine we drank, the words we stumblingly repeated, the air we breathed, the ground we walked across, were compounded of different stuff, part of the shredding sky and pounding sea, the *retzina* sloshing over the rims of copper beakers and the cards slapping down in strange, smoky little caverns.

Then suddenly it was over. We awoke to brisk blue days when to walk, to breathe, to move, was a conscious pleasure, when one could find the purest intoxication in light and air. Winds romped through the towns, raising dust eddies, snapping the small branches from the salt trees, setting loose shutters banging, whipping up the *gorgonas'* skirts, sending divers' caps skittering down the street or into the jumping harbour waters. Young girls walked with their hands tight on their skirts, and the young men loitered by the war memorial to watch them. Everything was alive, everything in motion — the rolling foliage of the salt trees and the bamboos swaying, the lively harbour and the jiggling boats, the snapping flags that tugged from swaying mast-heads, the priests trotting to the churches, head down, their black skirts flapping around their legs.

All the children were making kites now, kites of coloured paper and rag tails, and they raced with them along the *plateia* or climbed the mountains and loosed them over the valleys on two hundred yards of knotted string, aspiring to the blue and gleaming vault of heaven. High on the rocky crags the shepherd boys had them too, flying among the eagles.

It was a time of pure enchantment. No longer would the high wild cries of *'Afstralási! Afstralási!'* be flung from house to house whenever we appeared, no longer would the hundred children stream behind in a churning wake whenever we moved from the door. We were beginning to be accepted, although for our entire stay on the island there would continue to be loud cries of *'O Martis! Say!'* whenever the children appeared. At Emporio, Telendos, Vathy, Brosta, Piso, *'O Martis* and *Say!'* have, I think, become talismanic words.

Martin and Shane went to school now, a Greek school ominously but for no real reason named the 'Black School,' where not a single word of English was spoken even by the stout *Kyria I-Heraklia*, their teacher, and where Martin was reluctantly compelled to discard the beloved and familiar heroes of his imagination, Richard the Lion-heart, and the Black Prince and Joan of Arc and Robin Hood, for a new crop of strangely named *pallikaria* — Kolokotronis and Athanasios Thiakos and Miaolis and Boubalina. His intimacy with Achilles and Ajax and Hector and Agamemnon stood him in no real service. In Kalymnos the theme of heroism is direct, the historic memory a short one. The fighters against the Turks in the War of Liberation are the legendary giants. Troy fell more than three thousand years ago, and there are few small boys here who realise that their Kalymnian ancestors fought at Priam's embattled walls.

Martin and Shane trotted off to school happily with their friends at two o'clock every afternoon, each with a satchel, a tin cup, a thick slice of black bread and a half-*drachma tetrathio* ruled with thin blue lines. Their lessons seemed to be a friendly and casual business of a little writing, a little reading, and a lot of singing, games and gymnastics. Usually, if the day was a lovely one, lessons would be abandoned altogether and the whole school would pack up and go off on a picnic to Chorio or Brosta. The children would come singing home in the evening garlanded with yellow and white daisies threaded into floral chains and with scarlet anemones behind their ears and their arms full of bunches of almond blossom. They were ecstatically happy.

George and I were very happy too. If something of the dramatic quality of our first months had been dulled with the coming of spring and our own growing familiarity with the island and its people, we had found a new sense of consolidation and belonging. We had lost the feverish desperation that had marked both our flight from London and our arrival in Greece, and if the Fleet Street spectre still gibbered sometimes we did not let it worry us too much. An unpaid gas bill still pursued us politely from the Edgware Road. Because it was our only surviving link with our previous life we were loath to pay it. To it we developed a sentimental attachment that was never impaired as, month by month, its tone developed a sort of well-bred frigidity, a hint of querulousness, an overtone of curtness and, finally, a threat of legal action.

In those days of spring and early summer it was too important a symbol to be relinquished lightly. The monthly reminder of the smoke pall hanging over Paddington and the grey-brown rows of smutty terraces, of crowded subways and gas bills and income-tax and telephones and the shimmer of television screens, of the grey, anxious faces crowding the streets, of the feverish neuroses of staying alive and scrabbling for contentment, of the nightly retreats into private sorrows — in the polite reminders of all this coming from a gentleman incongruously named Fullalove we found deep cause for satisfaction.

The novel seemed to be going well. This was good. We were calm and easy in our work as we had not been for years, simply because time had ceased to be tyrannical. There was no sense of pace or pressure, none of that feeling of eternally trampling a treadmill which is the big city feel. There was no need to take benzedrine to stay awake or the barbiturates to go to sleep. We felt well — actually, physically, consciously well.

This came as something of a surprise. I had forgotten how good it was to breathe deeply, to walk miles without tiring, to be ravenously hungry. And although I remembered sometimes, a little wistfully, the comforts and conveniences of civilisation, I knew by experience that labour is not eliminated by gadgets, you can't get entertainment at the flick of a switch, nor comfort on the hire-purchase plan.

In Kalymnos we came to terms with time again. Although we worked hard, there was time left over — time to be a family, to play with the children, to walk, to talk for hours, to be still. I had an absurd wish to have a star map. It had been fifteen years since I had thought about the stars; I suppose I had even subconsciously taken the word to mean something of singular mammary development groomed by Hollywood. When we went to the Cinema Splendide in Kalymnos we went as one should go to the cinema, as one went as a child when the cinema was young — with a juvenile excitement and a sense of impending wonders. And even if it proved to be only an early Laurel and Hardy comedy with a scratched surface and a mute sound track, or some jerky melodrama that never made a quota, the sense of magical experience persisted. And there were half-*drachma* newspaper spills of sunflower seeds to be bought, and one would come out blinking and enchanted into the night and the smell of the sea and the tossing rush of the wind.

In the fullness and satisfaction of living hard and working hard there no longer seemed any reason to leave. Our earlier plan to take the results of our research to some more comfortable island and finish the manuscript in slightly more civilised surroundings was abandoned. The children were happy. We were living well and more cheaply, I imagine, than we could live anywhere else on earth. We had a great many friends of whom we were very fond. And, apart from all this, we both felt some queer sort of moral obligation to stay on until the sponge boats left for Africa. The divers had accepted us, and in their houses as well as in the *tavernas* we had received overwhelming hospitality. We had danced at their weddings, attended betrothals and held candles over the baptismal fonts of their children. Nobody ever suggested that we should, but we knew that we *had* to stand on the pier and wave farewell when the boats left.

With the coming of warmer weather and our more settled living conditions we began exploring the island. We worked for six days a week. Sunday was a declared and inviolate holiday. Usually we would pack a picnic and go across to Brosta or Merthies for the day, travelling on the island's solitary motor road in one of the ancient automobiles that serve here as buses — vintage vehicles of the kind my paternal grandmother from Huntingdon always referred to disdainfully as 'conveyances' when I was a child. Where all these Science Museum Buicks, Fords, Dodges, De Dion Boutons, Austins, Fiats and Chevrolets came from originally, and how they got here, remains one of the mysteries of Kalymnos — a mystery only less intriguing than the fact that they still go. Their doors are either hingeless or rusted fast to dented bodies. Old torn strips of cut genoa velvet, worn to the backing, cover broken springs. Cracked fragments of celluloid, brown and brittle, cling to the flapping window-frames. Often it is necessary to enter the car by climbing through the window, or to sit crouched forward, holding a door closed by the strength of your arm. There are invariably ten to fourteen passengers bundled into a car built to accommodate six, besides numerous birds, beasts, bundles, baskets and babies. Each car is hung prodigally with *ikons*, charms and talismans. One finds oneself accepting and implicitly trusting in their protective magic.

To ride across the island is an exhilarating experience, whizzing along through white walls, fruit trees, farms and hamlets, clattering past blue-washed churches and groves of silver olives with the canvas roof flapping above you and a broken spring jabbing beneath, a pig or a turkey plopped in your lap and the horn's melodious blast clearing the way of donkeys and goats and children and crones. I understand at last why Mr Toad fell in love with motoring.

In February the whole valley was a flood of almond blossom. It foamed around the old *castro* that the Knights of Rhodes had built and drifted high on every hill. The square white and blue

127

farmhouses were latticed across with moving shadows of the fig trees that surrounded them, and the bare stone-grey branches were already pricked with minute green leaves like little curled fists. The people were beginning to talk of *kalokairi*, of the full time of summer, when all the fruit would hang ripe on the trees. There would be figs and melons and grapes and the fruit of the prickly pear ... '*Sika, piponia, stafilia, fragosika ...*' They would chant it like a litany, their eyes shining.

At the village of Chorio, older and less Italianised than the port and huddled close beneath a dramatic purple and ochre crag desolately crowned with the walls and towers of a dead city far older yet, women came running down the blue-washed steps and alleys to bring us bunches of narcissus and hyacinth.

'Imagine the crocuses still frozen under the slush in Kensington Gardens,' George said. 'And all those dreary daffs in the window-boxes!'

Around Chorio the picture of the island's early movements is still clear. A mile up the road to the north, on a plateau gouged out by two deep, stony river beds that have not run water for centuries, is the very ancient city of Damos, where the Kalymnians had their citadel and fortress in the Heroic time. Sprawled over an area twice as great as that of Agamemnon's Mycenae, it is an impressive ruin, although no walls stand, nor gateways nor towers, and if you did not know what to look for you could walk across the hills and queer hummocks of spiky dun grass without noticing anything. For the houses of the Heroic time, heroically hewn from the living rock, have almost all been incorporated into the cottages or stables of the little farms strewn across the plateau. The wells of over three thousand years ago are still in use. Cyclopean blocks make gate posts or are built into walls, and the great retaining walls of the plateau look, at first glance, like another terrace for fig trees and grain crops.

You can still follow the original Sacred Way from Damos along the stony hillsides, skirting the tombs of the ancient kings, where fine jewellery of the Minoan style has been found, down to the ruined precincts of the Temple of Apollo, which lie just beside the main valley road a little beyond the village of Chorio. A hundred yards closer towards the village a second trail, no more than a rough goat-track, rises to the western rim of the valley, where the Dorian colonists of about 1,000 B.C. established their capital.

These cities were set well inland and on high places for fear of raiders from the sea. Their situations did not save them. Saracen marauders drove their inhabitants higher yet, to the grim, lonely crag that overhangs Chorio.

The dead city on the crag, abandoned now for more than five centuries to the bats and the lizards, is a queer, melancholy place. I thought at first that it reminded me a little of Mycenae, but it is only the nobility of the rock and the sweeping grandeur of its outlook that is the same. Mycenae is a sombre, brooding place, impregnated with blood and darkness, and a lingering echo of life. This city above Chorio is truly dead, as if the great earthquake of 1491 which finally toppled it destroyed even its memories. In the objective clarity of the early afternoon sunlight we toiled among the choked and tumbled stones, tracing the patterns of streets and the plans of houses. Walls still rise intact from the weeds, but one cannot connect them with dwelling-places, with cooking fires and supper smells and sleepy children and quarrelsome neighbours. The stones are dry, hot, colourless, chaotic; the weeds are rank. We found a huge underground cistern that still had water in it. Our faces were darkly and distantly mirrored within a circle of sky that floated on the blackness fifty feet below inside the rock. The pebbles we dropped seemed to fall for long seconds before any sound came, and then the whole great cavity bounded and boomed with the tiny dismal impacts magnified and multiplied into a terrible hollow rolling howl, as if we had unwittingly released the dead sorrows of centuries. We fled to the highest and furthest of the city walls (the top of the crag is like a tilted plate) and from the ruined battlements looked down a sheer precipice into a valley as sterile as the moon.

Yanni and Mikailis, who were with us, fidgeted and threw stones down into the valley. They had never been in the city before and didn't like it much. They were obviously oppressed by the loneliness and desolation, and were dying to drag us back to Chorio. Without too much reluctance we let ourselves be dragged, staying only to examine the twelve tiny white chapels planted in the ruined city — the only evident link with human beings.

Yet even the chapels are misleading. No one visits them any longer; the wreaths of flowers by the abandoned altars are as dry as bone, the few surviving *ikons* are cracked and peeling, the old Byzantine frescoes on the walls have been almost obliterated with damp. From the blotched, decaying walls mysterious faces peer dimly like pallid ghosts, less real than the clicking of the brown grasshoppers in the dry grass outside or the flick of the tiny arid-skinned lizards across the hot rocks.

Mikailis, with an air of defiance, picked up a piece of charcoal lying beside an old rusted censer and slowly and deliberately wrote his name in large black letters on the chapel wall among the peering painted faces. I deplored it but could understand that he felt it necessary at that moment to establish his identity. Then we passed again through the arched gateway and descended to the bright tumbled cubes of Chorio, following the trail that the survivors of the earthquake had trodden five hundred years ago when they came down into the valley and established their own town.

The pattern of that earlier architecture, the cubistic planes of the true Aegean houses, linked sometimes through the alleyways with shallow earthquake arches which make patterned tunnels of light and shade, has persisted through the centuries unaffected by outside influences. Chorio, like Pothia, is mostly blue, with a few houses painted yellow ochre, a few white. The touches on window-shutters and doors of pink and lime and cinnamon and grey are nothing short of miraculous. The blues range from the merest brightening of stark white, like a blue-rinsed sheet, to a thick, rich ultramarine. The variations on this one colour seem to be infinite, and combined with the subtle differences of wall textures, shapes, levels and the weathering effect of the sun, the blue sometimes produces fantastic optical illusions, particularly as the streets as well as the houses are covered with a thick coating of paint. Stairs melt into walls, corners curve, pavements swell into domed ovens. Sometimes there is no line of demarcation between house and sky, and walls soar up and thin out into pure atmosphere or the sky sweeps down to your feet, solidified, with two pink windows and a pot of red carnations drawn on. The black-clad women are exclamation points against the blue, their every movement emphatic, final, intuitively right, something completed and beautiful. Every scrap of colour sings — a boy's red jersey, an orange cat, a tray of poison-coloured sweets, a flower dropped on a twisted stair.

'If I could paint,' I say, needing at this moment to be Ben Nicholson and Picasso and Ben Shahn all rolled into one.

'Even if you could,' says George, 'no one would believe you.'

One Sunday we walked to the calm and lovely bay of Piso, following the donkey path that climbs up past the lonely white church of Agios Petros and cuts across the lichened uplands. Piso, like Chorio, follows the simple nomenclature of the island. Piso means 'back,' Chorio means 'country,' Brosta means 'front,' Elies means 'olives,' Merthies means 'myrtles,' Vathy means 'deep.'

At Piso we fished in the deep jewelled waters and cooked our lunch beside a fallen marble column among the fig trees that surround the doll's house church of the Panagyia. On the Sunday following, satisfied by our ability to clamber over stony mountains and having the children off our hands for the day (they having gone off to picnic with friends at Brosta), we at last attempted the steep and intimidating zig-zag trail — the Vathy trail — which, rising in almost perpendicular jaggedness above the port, had lured me ever since our arrival in Kalymnos. It took us two hours of strenuous climbing and the complete destruction of our London-made walking shoes before we got over the mountains and looked down on the broad green valley of Vathy, but it was worth it, not only for the restful beauty of the Vathy citrus groves, so green and cool and lush after the cruel and stony mountains, but for the compelling character of the mountains themselves. The high places have an awful, harsh beauty of their own, compounded of light and silence and the grim, enduring rock. There are no soft outlines, no shady places. These mountains are still and naked and terrible, not so much rejecting life as indifferent to it. For life *has* established a foothold even here. There are the tough, tangle herbs, clinging tenaciously to the bare stones, and queer lichens almost invisible in their colourless camouflage, and the stiff, short clumps of mountain grasses, and strange spiky plants — so much of the vegetation of the Greek landscape is composed of spikes — of an acid yellow colour and oozing an evil-smelling milk. And there are thyme and sage and *rigini* and rosemary and asphodel, and tall spikes of *alisfakia*, which the old women gather to make a green herb tea. And there are even flowers — minute coloured blooms no larger than pins' heads and yet with a Lilliputian perfection of pistil and petal and stamen — these are the *kookluthia*, the dolls' flowers. Spread with them over the stones are brittle juiceless flowers without colour that crumble when you touch them.

On the cliffs and precipices skinny sheep and goats forage for a few dry clumps of grass. Embossed on the thin blue sky a shepherd whistles them, and the air swings suddenly with bells — the true music of Greece. An old woman rises from the trail, dramatic and unexpected, her apron filled with herbs. A young, brown-legged girl bounds effortlessly over a stony ridge, leaping out of the sky with a dazzling tin milk can poised on her head. Two nuns plod placidly beside a donkey laden with brushwood and gorse. A hunter sits straddled on a high rock, his gun propped beside him. His cartridge belt is strung all round with green and yellow and crimson birds.

It would have been pleasant to make some of these excursions and expeditions by ourselves. We were beginning to feel the need for a little quietness, a few pauses for our own talk or for our own familiar, comfortable silences, a little relaxation from the task of trying to follow a new language, some occasional liberty from a way of life that was still foreign to us.

Sundays were the only days when a mutual solitude seemed possible.

But privacy is the state most difficult of all to attain in Greece, perhaps because the Greeks seem inherently incapable of understanding the need for it. Here, where families of ten or fifteen live in one room and sleep on one shelf, people are accustomed from birth to a communal existence. There is a highly complex and delicate balance of personal relations between families and neighbours, who are obliged by their very poverty to live in such propinquity that the whole of everyone's actions, and almost all his thoughts, are open to the inspection of the rest.

The men carry this communal existence to the coffee-house and *taverna* — how seldom one sees one of them drinking alone — and the women have the intimate gossip shops and workrooms of the narrow sunny streets, which they share companionably. It is here that they carry the little tin stoves, the washtubs, the spindles of wool, the nursing babies. Even the clumsy wooden looms, which must necessarily be permanent indoor fixtures, are set up close to an open window, not for the light that might facilitate the work but so that even while the housewife weaves she remains part of the life of the street.

Excepting at night, when doors and windows are barred against evil spirits and the dangerous humour of darkness, the little Kalymnian houses are wide open for everyone to see and to enter at will.

I think this must always have been so. The Romans leave private villas. The Greeks leave only temples and markets. Only the communal buildings are constructed to endure, for it is only here that their true life centres. It may be that it is necessary to sacrifice privacy in order properly to understand the art of living together, as the Greeks in many ways have understood it better than any civilisation on earth.

But for us, products of a social structure that puts a high value on an individual right to solitude, it was, and is, difficult to surrender ourselves to a community. And in our early days it often became a matter of desperation.

We never did, in fact, find privacy on our Sunday expeditions.

No matter how secretive we were, how cautiously we set out, how nonchalantly we might distribute our food bundles through

133

our pockets so that they would not be seen, as if to pretend we were just taking a stroll down the *plateia*, we could never move more than fifty yards before Manolis, or Mikailis, or Yanni (or more usually all three) would materialise from a café table or from behind a tree, or stroll out from an alley, or shin down from a balcony and confront us with gentle, inquiring smiles.

'Eeeeh! Where are *you* going?'

'Oh, just a little walk. Up the trail there.'

'*Parme.* Let's go.'

'But haven't you something else to do?'

'Nothing, nothing!' And after a while, very earnestly, 'Look, you tell me when you want to go somewhere. It isn't right for you to have to go alone.'

Once, out of pure desperation, George said pointedly, 'Listen, I don't think it's a good thing for you to leave your wives and families *every* Sunday.'

Evidently conscious of the note of censure in this, Mikailis and Yanni dropped behind, whispering together. Then after a time, when we thought we had shaken them off, Mikailis went loping back along the *plateia* and Yanni hurried to overtake us.

'We sit now and have a cup of coffee,' he said.

'We've just had coffee,' George protested.

Yanni steered us resolutely to a café table. By the time we had finished our coffees Mikailis had reappeared. He was heading down the street towards us, and behind him in single file came his wife Irini, looking a little puzzled, Yanni's wife Polymnea, looking resentful, and their ten assorted children.

'*Parme!*' said Yanni happily, confident that there could be no further cause for objection. 'Now we will all go together!'

After that we never rebelled openly again. Indeed it would have been folly to do so, for Yanni developed an espionage system which Himmler would have envied. His disconcerting power to materialise anywhere and at any time would have cowed the most rebellious spirit. If I walked along the cliffs to read a magazine quietly for half an hour, or to worry out some elusive passage of the book, he was there within two minutes. If we fled furtively at night to enjoy a brief solitude in the moonlight at the end of the breakwater his murmured '*Kalispera*' would come floating out of the night before we had time to sit down. Often, with uncanny intuition, he had already established himself at a destination we had foolishly believed to be secret, and his smile of welcome would have a faint flavour of reproof, as if we were children caught red-handed in an act of mischief by a tolerant father. We gave in meekly and allowed ourselves to be guided. In any case it was impossible to move anywhere without six or eight of Shane's or Martin's friends trotting purposefully behind. Whatever one did there was always a silent figure or an attentive group watching with a dumb and patient absorption. When we took stock at the end of six months and realised that in all that time there had not been a single night when there had been only the two of us together, we accepted it with a sort of numb resignation, as if our sense of privacy had at last been anaesthetised.

Angela, in the next house but one, was extravagantly pregnant at the time, and rigidly house bound. She had a wistful regret that she was incapable of climbing on the gregarious bandwagon. 'Even if it *is* a boy,' she would say, 'I wish I wasn't having this baby just now. I'd love to take you around, instead of you having to go with all that poor lot tagging along.'

And she used to say: 'I never see you without a dozen kids hanging on to your skirts. If you like them that much you ought to make some more of your own.' Angela's thoughts were naturally obsessed with maternity at the time.

With her husband Georgios the grocer, and her younger sister Maria, Angela lived above the barber's shop on the corner of the *plateia*. Both sisters, although Kalymnian by birth, had been reared in High Holborn, the London area where most expatriate Greeks seem to congregate. When their mother died their father brought them back to Kalymnos for a holiday, so they might become better acquainted with that vast and intricate web of relationships that every Kalymnian child inherits at birth — aunts, uncles, cousins and in-laws of first, second, third and even fourth remove. Angela was wooed and won by the handsome grocer Georgios, and after returning to London to settle up her affairs she came back to Kalymnos the following year, bringing with her Maria, her trousseau and numerous purchases from Selfridge's. With their father they all settled into the little house Angela's grandfather had built. Maria had never intended to stay more than a couple of months, but her father became ill, Angela became pregnant, and Maria stayed on and on, dealing with each new crisis as it arose.

It is something of a tight squeeze in the house on the corner, because it is a respectable middle-class house, rather ornate and, like ours, improbably lozenged. It lacks the convenience of the big bedshelf that easily accommodates the families of the poor. Being middle class, Angela and her husband must sleep in a double bed with a veneered walnut headboard, which takes up all the available space of the tiny second room. Maria is relegated to a camp bed in the sitting-room, and the father, while he remained alive, was consigned to a small and practically airless loft.

This passion for respectable, 'proper' furniture makes for a great deal of discomfort in the homes of the middle classes. In the poor houses a family of ten can live quite comfortably in one room, even with an illusion of spaciousness. Angela's house has two rooms, a landing and a loft — but every square inch of floor space and wall space is so crammed with curtains and carpets and furniture and such a clutter of vases and glassware and dishes and bric-à-brac that once inside the house it is very difficult indeed to get out again.

There are innumerable chairs ranged around the walls of the tiny sitting room, and a stiff-backed sofa upholstered in burgundy and gold to match the upholstery of the inner circle of chairs mathematically spaced around an enormous table standing bang in the centre of the room. The curtains, draped heavily over every window so that neither light nor air can enter, are also gold — an imitation brocade that is doubly prized because Angela brought it all the way from Selfridge's in Oxford Street. On the large, tricky sideboard are arranged convoluted vases of delicately shaded pink and blue glass, shells and sponges and pebbles, ash-trays from English seaside resorts and framed photographs of the girls who used to work with Angela and Maria in the London clothing factory. Above the sideboard Elizabeth of England, in diamond tiara and the broad blue ribbon of the Garter, looks down with a well-bred lack of surprise at the frequent gatherings of Angela's female relatives and in-laws — ancient, high-stomached women who sit with folded hands on the sofa or the high-backed chairs, or with an erect immobility on Maria's camp bed, their faces still and dark and expressionless, like an occult frieze, but their eyes very watchful. They are intent on catching Angela out in some breach of Kalymnian etiquette.

On these occasions Angela, as is proper to her position as the young matron, takes the centre chair between the windows. It is Maria, twenty-two and virgin still, who runs backwards and forwards from the kitchen with bowls of preserves and trays of coffee, thick and black and sweet. It is Maria who scurries out to borrow a kilo of sugar. It was Maria who scuttled up the loft ladder and mysteriously shushed the petulant old man's cries. It is Maria who shoves a bottle of camomile water into the open howling mouth of the baby swaddled in a cot in the corner beneath the manly, confident gaze of Philip, Duke of Edinburgh.

It is Maria who picks up little Thoxouli and changes her eternally dripping drawers.

'Sometimes,' Maria says grimly, 'I wish we'd never come for that bloody holiday!'

We are very fond of The Girls. Angela, in spite of her carefully hoarded copies of the *Daily Mirror* and *Woman's Day* and her nostalgic dreams of sizzling pork sausages with bacon and Lyons Corner Houses and jellied eels and Ramsgate Sundays and Odeons as big as palaces, must inevitably settle into the prescribed pattern of the Kalymnian *yieneka*. With her Greek parentage, her religious training and her strong sense of the superstitious, she has no weapons to fight with. Maria, however, has no ties of husband and family and one day might conceivably 'up and off' back to High Holborn. She retains her salty Cockney humour and can more easily remain amusedly detached from the Kalymnian way of life. Both of them have a typical urban curiosity about the 'queer goings-on' here and are alternately shocked, startled, overcome with superstitious awe or collapsed into fits of wildest giggling.

For this reason they are a wonderful source of information. If something seems odd to them they know it will interest me, and they run in obligingly to tell me about it.

It was in Angela's house that I first attended a *Koliva* session, on the second anniversary of the death of her mother. 'Come in and have a look,' Maria urged. 'It's ever so interesting.'

Koliva, in the strict sense, is the food of the dead. It is a sort of dry pudding made with wheat, sugar, cinnamon, almonds, currants and spices. It is prepared only on the stipulated anniversaries of family deaths or on the day of each year set aside for the soul of all the dead. Once its ingredients included pomegranate seeds. *Koliva* is made three days after a bereavement, prepared again on the ninth day, then the fortieth, at the end of three, six, nine and twelve months and, thereafter, once a year on the death anniversary. On the days for All Souls every family, excepting only brides of less than a year, makes *Koliva*.

The basic pudding is prepared by the housewife according to a rigidly established ritual. The wheat must be carefully washed three times, the currants twice. The almonds must be blanched in boiling water from a clean pot. Throughout every operation the housewife must constantly wash her hands so that no speck of dirt can soil the snowy whiteness of the sifted sugar. When everything is cooked and mixed in a huge bowl, friends and relatives are invited to watch the *Koliva* being decorated by one of the ancient crones who are the professional experts at the art. Until a year or so ago the invitation to attend *Koliva* was formal. Special buns were baked and sent around on a tray to the houses of intended guests. If a bun was taken the invitation was accepted. Now word of mouth is sufficient.

As I expected, the *Koliva* session was strictly *yienekas* only. There were perhaps twenty women squeezed into Angela's little sitting-room, and at the centre table a very old lady, shrouded in shawls, sat crouched over the dish of *Koliva*. She had covered it entirely with finely ground white sugar, smoothed with her new white paper until it was a perfectly symmetrical mound. Then, using another clean piece of paper with an ornate cross drawn on it, she pricked the pattern through on to the sugar with a needle that had been washed in boiling water. All round the room the other women were sorting almonds and currants into perfectly matched sizes in little saucers that also had been scalded in boiling water. The old *gorgona*, who was tetchy and fussy, used the currants and almonds to fill in the pattern of the cross and to make a border of stylised flowers around the edge of the mound.

Angela, bulging hugely, poor love, in her best brown morocain, explained apologetically that this was not a very elaborate *Koliva* because her mother had been dead for two years, and besides, what with Thoxouli to attend to and the baby coming and all … The rich, she said wistfully, used expensive silver lozenges of various shapes instead of plebeian currants and almonds. They literally covered the *Koliva* with decoration. 'Simply lovely, it is,' adds Angela, who has much wistfulness but no envy. Maria, rushing about with trays of coffee and sweet little biscuits she had been all the morning baking, grins sardonically and blows the tumbled hair out of her eyes.

'Ah, the rich like to keep the poor in their places,' she says, 'even after they're dead.'

When the *Koliva* is finished — and even a simple *Koliva* will take hours to prepare — it is flanked by two tall candles and left all night in some conspicuous place (presumably so that the dead soul will have no trouble in finding it) with a glass of cold water beside it. In the morning, at the first ringing of the church bells, it is taken to the church and placed on a table with burning candles thrust into the soft sugar crust. The name of the dead person is read out and blessed; the priest takes a spoonful of the *Koliva* and eats it. It is then carried from the church and taken in solemn procession to the cemetery. There a spoonful is sprinkled on the grave of the dead person. The rest is taken through the streets of the town by an old woman employed for the purpose. She must go from house to house and shop to shop, offering a little of the *Koliva* on a silver spoon to every person she sees.

Koliva is, in fact, a delicious confection, and all of us have developed a passion for it. The four of us sit with our mouths open obediently whenever an old woman with a basin passes by.

On the mass *Koliva* days each church is a wonderful sight, for there are hundreds of these beautifully decorated plates aglitter with silver and candles. Afterwards swarms of children fight and leap outside to see who can eat the most.

The first *Koliva* session at Angela's cleared up something that had been mystifying me for some weeks. Shane had had her sixth birthday a little before this, and old Leonidas the cake vendor had made for her an 'English' cake, which was ushered to the house wrapped carefully in a clean white cloth like a religious object. A little card pinned to it said, in laboriously printed capitals, HAPPY RETURNS THE BIRTHDAY FROM LEONIDAS.

In accordance with Shane's demands the cake was then iced with white frosting and, seeing some pretty silver balls and lozenges in a jar in the sweet-shop window, I bought them and contrived a pattern of flowers and leaves on top of the frosting.

The only candles to be had in Kalymnos are church candles. I bought six slim yellow tapers and placed them carefully round the cake. It looked very pretty.

After all this trouble I was a little put out and hurt by the fact that not one of Shane's small barefooted guests would touch a crumb of it. They kept crossing themselves fervently and asking if it was for the rabbit — a question calculated to humiliate even the most tolerant housewife! It was a long time before I realised that they had all — none of them ever having seen a birthday cake before, since Greek children have no birthdays — taken it to be *Koliva* for the Animus, gone to his mountain grave forty days past!

12

Notes from a journal. Coming home from the *taverna* encounter Maria, down by the sea emptying a bucket. Angela has at last given birth. Alas, alas, another girl! Maria very tired and shaking with high excitement. A note of hysteria in her giggles. 'Cor! you should have seen old Katerina, hanging over the bed with her tongue out, twisting her great head this way and that to try and get a better look. And everyone jabbering and screaming and bawling.'

'How about Angela?'

Maria giggles. 'She was doing her own bawling! What's the name of that stuff? You know, the stuff that comes out after? Horrible looking, it is. Placenta? Is that it? Yes, I suppose that's it. Well, they're a suspicious lot here, and you're supposed to take it right away and bury it somewhere. Can't throw it in the sea, or anything. I've been right up the mountain tonight with that stuff in a paper bag. Dug a hole up near Agios Vassilias. Talk about laugh! Stumbling all over the mountain, I was!'

She rinses the bloody bucket and stretches herself wearily. 'Better get back now and start soaking the sheets.' We suggest that it's all good practice and that she'll be an old hand by the time she gets round to having her own babies. She shoots us a look that is pure poison. 'The day you catch me letting myself in for *that* you can lock me up in the loony-bin!'

Baby revolting. Huge. Looks like a fullback. Covered with black hair and its head wrapped up in a turban. Swaddled up in Thoxouli's cot, and the cot hung with crosses, medallions, amulets. Angela prone on the camp stretcher, still looking enormous. Soggy with exhaustion, guilt, relief, disappointment. Elizabeth of England smiling graciously down. Husband gone off to shop in a fury. Parents-in-law furious too. Midwife old crone in usual greasy black skirt and head-scarf. Take one look at her fingernails and am nearly sick. Feel terribly sorry for Angela and sit for a long time so she can describe every detail of her labour. Describes it. Makes her feel chirpier to have an interested audience. Later climb up the mountain to try to find some flowers for her. Find a handful of white irises, the very first, among the weeds and nettles close to Agios Vassilias. Bring them back to her and she weeps a little. 'You know what it's like,' she sobs, but I don't — not this way. Think of my own glamorous birthings, flowers, visitors, George tight as a tick, private room, private bath, nurses running in and out, all starched and white, and everybody so glad for me. Sitting with poor Angela crying over five white irises, I feel like crying too.

'*They're a suspicious lot!*' Realise Maria means superstitious. The baby's umbilical cord, like the placenta, must be taken away and buried secretly. Sympathetic magic? The mother must not receive visitors other than closest family for nine days, and those visitors she has must never praise the baby, for fear of the evil eye and malevolent spirits. (No likelihood of the family's praising the poor ugly little thing. It's female.) Angela not allowed to move from house for forty days, nor go to church, because she is 'unclean.' On the first Sunday after forty days she may stand outside the church door with the baby in her arms, but not go inside. At the end of the service priest comes to door, sprinkles her with holy water and takes the child inside the church. She may then meekly follow him in. If the child is a boy it's taken behind the altar. If a girl, it's dumped on the altar steps and left for the mother to pick up. All practices traceable more easily through the *Golden Bough* than through *Holy Bible*.

Ante-natal care is terrifyingly primitive. For instance: where in a hospital they would use a breast pump, here an aged and toothless crone is employed for same purpose. Angela's eyes still wide with mingled disgust and fascination. 'You put a clean napkin around her neck, and she gets down on her knees by the side of the bed. Of course you make sure she washes her mouth out first. It's ever such a queer feeling — I just didn't know where to look!' Angela calls her breasts 'me chests.'

Try very gently to interest her in modern systems, regular feeding hours. Know even as I talk that I'm wasting my time. Thoxouli being breast fed a month before this one was born. By the end of the week baby will have a dummy stuck in its mouth and be picked up and fed every time it cries. Normal here for babies still to be breast fed when aged two, even three years. Story goes that Anastasis, one of labourers in the town, big cheerful husky man, was still being breast fed when seven years old. Coming home from game of football to mother's cornucopian bosom. Even Kalymnians seem to regard this as going a bit too far.

'It's not much of a life here for a woman,' poor Angela says. 'I know I'll have another next year, and the year after, and every year until I make a boy!'

Like to plant an Odeon right outside her door. Like to supply her with Lyons Swiss Rolls in plastic wraps and thick pork sausages every day of her life. Like to write a letter to Elizabeth of England in her diamond tiara and blue sash of the Garter.

13

'Who? Who? Who?' the dwarf ghosts squeaked. '*Pios?Pios?Pios?*' There was one hopping frog-fashion at my feet. Two more dangled from the dusky branches of the salt tree that overhung the darkening coffee tables, a fourth whirled insanely among the potato baskets at the top of the blue steps that led to Calliope's corner shop.

Whirling too, with the hopping one tugging at my skirt, I guessed great and improbable personages — beasts, birds, the comic characters of folklore — until the two ghosts in the salt tree dropped through the branches and rolled on the pavement in a thrashing tangle of brown and dirty legs and jerking hummocks of off-white sheeting.

'And what is Sevasti going to say when she sees those sheets?'

Martin's scarlet, sweaty face emerged briefly to reassure me. 'They're not *our* sheets.' Georgouli's mother had dressed them up. It was quite all right, *she* had said.

'Ah, never mind, *Kyria*. The sheets are old. And it's Carnival.' Georgouli's mother was serving coffee at the tables set out on the white painted squares next to Manolis Klonaris' strip of pavement, paying no attention whatever to the small scarecrow figure that shadowed her and mocked every gesture. Only the twigs of arms in the familiar striped jersey sleeves were recognisable. The rest was nightmarish — a woman's flannel nightgown stuffed beneath with pillows, an upturned basket crowning it.

'A glass of water. Quickly now Georgouli!' She gave the order without turning round, and the nightgown lurched away with a dreadful sort of mincing limp, its basket head waggling provocatively. At the tables the divers slapped their thighs and hooted like cruel children. Georgouli's mother hooted too, holding up her hand, as she always did, to cover the gaping toothless hole of her mouth. And then she limped along a few steps, deliberately exaggerating the mincing waggle of her crippled walk to demonstrate the cleverness of her son's mimicry.

Another woman — perhaps the twentieth that day — passed through the tables with *Koliva*. We took our spoonfuls and blessed the dead, for this Saturday in the middle of Carnival was set aside for All Souls.

'Do you make Carnival like this in Australia?' they asked eagerly, and I thought of the girls in tights at the artists' ball and the shuffling crowds milling in the streets on New Year's Eve. No, we didn't make Carnival like this in Australia, I said, nor, as far as I knew, anywhere else in the world.

The Carnival at this stage had already been in progress for two weeks and would continue for a week longer, culminating in a wild day of feasting and dancing on the threshing floor at Brosta before the rigorous forty-day fast of Lent. The period of Carnival is called *Apokriés* (literally, 'abstain from meat'), and there are several *apokréo* fast days in the Orthodox year. At Carnival time the word has come to have exactly the opposite of its literal meaning and, for the first two weeks at least, indulgence rather than abstention is the rule. It is, anyway, for those who can afford to buy meat. And even for the poor it is one of the four occasions in the year when a traditional satiation with meat can be enjoyed — the others are Christmas, Easter and Saint George's Day.

At any rate, from our point of view there seemed to have been feasting enough. There had been many weddings. On the previous Sunday there had been eight we had been obliged to attend, and we had staggered from party to party through the night until our heads thrummed and throbbed with the wine and the smoke and the songs and our feet refused to shuffle another circle of the wedding dance, yet somehow shuffled, anyway. Because how could one offend that drawn, wax-white pair of effigies, staring-eyed beneath their wilted garlands, hours past the point where offence might be noticed? (We must dance and dance, and they must suffer it until the last unendurable moment, for that was the established order of things. And we danced in praise of the great, deep, dammed, straining life force that would burst now and engulf them — poor exhausted children! And we danced to propitiate Aphrodite, the Cyprian, cackling in the corner over greedy pickings of dogfish, with oil trickling down her hairy chin on to the loosened ends of a greasy black scarf, her lascivious old eyes bright with malice.)

There had been many christenings during Carnival too. I can no longer remember how many tiny naked Marias and Annas and Constantines and Alexanders and Fotinis had been plunged red and squalling into the gigantic brass font that must have been lugged for miles that week from house to house, up the mountains and down again, but one will serve for all, since a Kalymnian baptism differs only in degree from house to house, and the christening of Katerina's baby might have been any one of a dozen others.

In the Greek Orthodox Church baptism is not only one of the great mysteries, but has both a mystical and secular significance which the outsider can scarcely comprehend. Quite apart from religious considerations, omission of baptism would be unthinkable to any Greek on purely material grounds. It is the guarantee of his validity as a human being. Without it he does not exist. To obtain his voter's registration he must produce his certificate of baptism. Without it in adult life he is ineligible for civic duties, public office, even normal employment. Until the actual moment of immersion he does not even possess a name.

The service itself, in the form of the Divine Liturgy, has remained totally unchanged since it was written by St John Chrysostom towards the end of the fourth century. It still retains all the dark and thrilling drama of a soul being girt and armed miraculously in the very presence of the dreadful spirits who would snatch it if they could. It is the true drama of Christianity in its infancy as an accepted religion — Christianity emerging from the Catacombs into the light of day. The Cross is a living symbol, as though Constantine were still rapt with his vision of the flaming shape in the sky. *'By this sign conquer!'* And his mother Helena is kneeling in an ashpit on the Hill of Golgotha, the sweet spiced smell of basil in her nostrils and her white hands fearful on the splintered grey wood. The Cross! The Sign!

Katerina is Sevasti's niece, a thin, silvery girl with a look of illness about her and a wry, acidulous manner refreshing in a place where women are normally docile. She is just nineteen. She has been married two years to a diver everyone likes, Georgios, a short and powerfully built young man with a very sweet smile and a confident thrust to his sleek, round head. Their first child is a girl. Neither of them seems to mind particularly. The party is as lavish as if it had been a firstborn boy.

'Maybe it would be different,' Sevasti cannot resist the aside, 'if it were her fifth girl instead of the first.'

Katerina and Georgios live in a large blue cube at the base of the medieval castle of the Knights of Rhodes, not far from Sevasti's very much smaller cube. Three round towers of weathered stone that look like ancient watchtowers but are, in fact, disused windmills climb up behind the house, which in an otherwise barren area is prettily surrounded by almond and fig trees.

By the time we arrive the evening smells rich and strong of hot meat and oil and garlic, and there is great activity in the house and around it. Children are clambering in every almond tree, stuffing their mouths and pockets with little furry green nuts. Half a dozen women bustle in and out of the kitchen and up and down the outside staircase, carrying chairs and tables and jugs and covered trays and great dishes of sticky-looking sweatmeats. Costas Manglis, faintly flushed with wine and exertion, is helping Georgios to manhandle the great brass font from Saint Stephanos up the stairs and into the top room.

Captain Miches and young Captain Charlie, who are standing as godfathers, are lining up big wicker jars of *retzina* outside the kitchen door.

In the top room — blue walls and one of the lovely old bamboo ceilings and an entire lithographed set of the adventures of Genovefa — at least a hundred people are packed already. Children and old women squat and recline and lean along the bedshelf, peering through the railings. The rest sit circle within circle on the borrowed chairs around the centrepiece of the great font. Kerosene lamps hang from the walls among the lithographs and icons and yellowed photographs, and a great Tilly lamp hisses a dazzling white light from the centre of the ceiling. The room is unbearably hot.

The priests and musicians arrive together, all puffing from the climb. The chief figure is the old priest from Saint Stephanos, a cigarette puffing furiously in the middle of a beard like a white feather boa. His skirts are hitched up over the big climbing shepherd's boots he always wears. His assistant is a pale, ascetic young priest with glossy hair and liquid eyes and a fine beard, black and curly. He carries the holy oil and wine and scissors and candles. (The scissors dangle from a piece of knotted string; the oil and wine are in those familiar containers reading Bon Ton Cheese Corn — An Appetising Snack.)

Led by the gigantic figure of Captain Miches, awkward and sheepish-looking in the crowded room, the official party comes up from the kitchen: Georgios looking pale and proud, young Captain Charlie blushing shyly, Katerina carrying the baby with Sevasti's daughters surrounding her like stately figures from an old frieze. Bringing up the rear comes a procession of women with water jars, three filled with hot water and three with cold. Under the supervision of the old priest, who has donned a faded surplice over his black robe (it looks rather like a floral pinafore), the water is poured into the font. At intervals he tests the temperature of the water with his elbow, as efficient as any good nanny, his sleeves rolled high over his thin, old, white arms. The young priest hands lighted candles to the children. His glossy knot of hair has come undone. It falls down his back in a long shining twist. Georgios knots it up for him, inexpertly, and they grin at each other.

Captain Miches thrusts out his huge hands, and Katerina hands him the baby. Young Captain Charlie shuffles up beside him to hold the fringe of its shawl. Their black peaked divers' caps are pushed back on their heads, and their foreheads are shining with sweat. The old priest has found his spectacles somewhere under the flap of the floral pinny. Crossly he shushes the audience and opens the little red book. There is a sudden silence, and then the words of fifteen centuries ago burst from the old priest's lips in a chant that is shrill and strange and electrifying ... The Cross! The Sign ...

The sign is protecting Kate Ana's baby now. Captain Miches and young Captain Charlie turn their backs on the font. They turn very slowly and gravely and spit three times in the direction of the bedshelf, where the devil and his attendant malevolencies must be lurking among the nodding old ladies and the wide-eyed, unsuspecting children who are singeing one another's hair with lighted tapers. The two captains stare solemnly into the crowded darkness.

The old priest is making the sign of the Cross over the gently steaming water in the great brass bowl with a tiny vial of holy water, with his own bobbing head, with his thin trembling hand. At intervals, while the low sing-song chant of the young priest rises and falls, the old man waggles his head in the sign of the Cross close to the baby's face. It is very intimate and charming. It is a wonderful game. The baby crows and laughs as the fine white feathers of his beard whisk across her face.

It still seems to be a game as she is swung suddenly out of the shawl, out of Captain Miches' great enfolding arms, up and up past the floating white feathers and high into the smoke and the empty heat and the incense smell — a little pink piece of meat stiff with sudden terror. Or does she smell the devil near? Quickly! Quickly! There is a concerted gasp of urgency as the old priest plunges her down, down into the steaming water in the font, into the water crossed and recrossed with the Sign. With one hand he holds her under; the other hand frequently makes the sign of the cross again and again over the churning water. And then the child is swung clear again and high, and the wail comes on this second upward swing, a great shocked bellow that bursts into a room breathless with relief. The poor little thing is purple now, with rage, perhaps, or realisation that this is no game at all, but a deadly serious business.

Up and down, up and down, plunging and writhing and kicking, she is ducked and dipped and crossed and held aloft, and ducked and dipped again. The old *papas* is dripping. His sleeves have come down and fallen into the font. Captain Miches and young Captain Charlie move in closer, holding in stiffly extended arms the snowy new cloth that will catch the poor purple screaming scrap. They look huge and determined. No devil, one feels, would stand a chance against them. The lids of the Bon Ton Cheese Corn cans have become stuck. The young priest struggles with them, and Georgios rushes in to help as the baby is flung into the cloth. The glossy coil of hair goes snaking down the young priest's back again.

The baby no longer screams. It gasps a little, and its tiny chest heaves and shudders spasmodically as the Sign is marked on its naked flesh — in oil and in wine, on its back and its breast and its feet and hands. It is all very, very thorough and earnest. The young priest moves in with the scissors on the old piece of knotted string. From the baby's head little draggled wisps of black down are clipped, forehead, nape, left side and right. Katerina bows as she offers the new clothes to be blessed. Miches' big clumsy hands fumble with the delicate fastenings of a thin gold chain. The cross looks like a tiny living sign in gold, embossed on the baby's flesh …

And then they are moving around the font in a circling procession, half dancing, half prancing. The two priests are in the lead, and their chanting is high and strange and richly exuberant. Suddenly everyone in the room gives a high, wild shout of triumph. It is like a sharp nail run down your spine. Katerina, weeping, stumbles forward to kiss the hands of Captain Miches and young Captain Charlie. Everyone is laughing and shouting at once, a dozen women are vociferously contesting the right of bundling up the baby (who now appears to be mercifully unconscious) and carrying her downstairs to the little hammock over the bedshelf in the lower room. The two priests are washing their hands in an enamel basin — one is reminded, strangely, of two surgeons who have completed a dangerous and delicate operation. There is the smell of strong green soap and clean towels.

The baby is borne away, a blue bead pinned to its blanket to ward off the evil eye ... Anna, daughter of Georgios and Katerina, by the grace of God now Christian — and safe ...

The two priests are struggling out of their surplices; the old man has his cigarette alight before he even begins to wring out his sodden sleeves. Sevasti's girls are coming with trays of little glasses of *strega* and *ouzo* and slabs of honey cake on coloured paper napkins. Katerina, smiling through her tears and white with exhaustion, is pinning tiny gold crosses fixed to pink ribbon bows on to lapels and shirt fronts and dresses. Sevasti pushes through the crush and hugs me tightly because she is overcome with the beauty and mystery of what has just happened, and she cannot convey it to me in any other way.

'Next we shall baptise Martin and Shane,' she whispers, bursting with love. 'Make them truly Greek children.'

Shane's horrified pink face peers over the taper she has been holding. 'Mummy, it's without *knickers*!'

Shane has lately become modest.

My cross is The Waltz.

I began with a completely hostile attitude towards this dance, I think because of a story my mother used to tell of my grandmother Sara Carson, who, according to family legend, was a tragically beautiful Irish-Jewess with a hand so small that she could put it right inside the lamp chimney to clean it, and who won waltzing competitions in a rose taffeta dress with a glass of water balanced on her lovely head and eggshells on the heels of her dancing slippers.

As a healthy, growing girl with hands which always seemed as big as plates and an unrivalled capacity for awkwardness, this sort of story was the stuff of intimidation. I could not break an egg into a bowl without munching up the shell into a pulp. There was no question of putting them on my heels and dancing. Yet sometimes I used to peer through the window of the Oddfellows' Hall on Saturday nights and it seemed to me strange that such ordinary dull adults could twirl and swing with such ease and confidence against the background of paper streamers and hydrangea tubs. Although neither glasses of water nor eggshells were involved, it didn't *look* all that difficult.

This was during the middle 'thirties and everyone knew that all the poetry of movement was contained in those deceptively simple steps — that to dance The Waltz was to float in a dream. It was the Period of *Vienna Nights*, of films about Strauss. And the Danube flowed around the world.

The allure was there, but my attitude to waltzing had always been defensive. I had tried it only a couple of times — once at a High School dance with a broken-nosed fifth-year boy whom I worshipped with a depth of passion that even now can make me shudder with retrospective agony. We completed three or four stumbling circles, and I remember his telling me he would probably join the air force after the exams. Then he surrendered me without protest, or even a backward glance, to a lumpish boy in my own class who was very good at Latin. I attempted it again, years later, with a Hungarian who had Charles Boyer eyes and the trick, at every completed circle, of trying to lift me right off my feet. Possibly he too had memories of *Vienna Nights*, or maybe it was just that girls were wraiths in Budapest.

After that I rather shied off the waltz and slid gratefully into the easy night-club shuffle that went with the tight black dresses and thick mascara I had come to affect.

With George the problem of the waltz had never arisen. It was something he did not care about one way or the other, although he had a quiet pride in the rumba he had learned from a beautiful brunette on the Starlight Roof to the music of Xavier Cugat.

The Kalymnians, even had they been aware of my waltzing inhibitions, probably would have ignored them. No sooner would

I wriggle forward to take my place in the circle, eager to fling myself into the riotous abandon of one of the Kalymnian dances, than some great diver in black cap and high-necked jersey would toss a ten-*drachmae* bill to the *bouzouki* player with a shouted injunction. I would be seized in a grip that defied escape, and everyone else would retire from the tiny floor space to watch the waltz.

Oh, for grandmother Sara's eggshells here!

Half the time my feet are not on the floor at all, and the other half they are beneath a pair of stomping sea boots. Since the dancing area is never much more than three or four feet in diameter my flying legs create havoc among the innermost circle of the astonished onlookers. We stop for a second or two so that my partner may refresh himself with a glass of *retzina*. Sometimes he hastily grabs one for me too. Perhaps my mother was mistaken and it was strong liquor the beautiful Sara carried on her head for just such a contingency! Then I am flung away again, whirled into the air, stomped over, lifted and tossed and twirled until the man with the *bouzouki* judges that we have had our ten-*drachmae* worth.

Tonight I dance with Heracles, for it is Captain Miches who is using me to demonstrate the waltz. 'I was all right, eh?' he grins happily when I have finally collapsed onto the nearest chair to wild shouts of approval. 'We will dance this again later. I think it is good. But now we will go and eat.'

We eat in the kitchen, beside a bedshelf littered with exhausted old ladies and children who cannot stand the pace any longer. There are five hammocks slung above it. In the smallest baby Anna, pink as a rose, is asleep, safe from all devils.

Katerina and Georgios are waiting on the guests. Only men may sit at the big round table which is piled with plates of meat and fish and *dolmadhes* and octopus and squid and potatoes and fried eggs and enough bread for an army. Miches and young Captain Charlie, the godfathers and therefore the principals of the occasion, are served like kings. Sevasti has appointed herself personal assistant to George — her daughters have taken over the two captains — and George is trying, between forkfuls of food, to learn the words of *Psarapoula* under the energetic tuition of half a dozen divers. How the children can sleep and the old ladies can snore through it I cannot imagine. Above our heads the wooden ceiling shakes and shudders to the stamping of dancing feet, and there is a fine rain of dust over the table. Occasionally a large lump of plaster falls. Nobody pays any attention. Sevasti has a wild stare in her eyes as she studies two bottles — one of *retzina* and one of paraffin. It is clear a few minutes later that she has mixed them up. Nobody pays any attention to that either. *Psarapoula* roars on … *Yakara sas pallikaria, apto ialo* … The glasses are banging on the table and the sea boots pounding. Someone climbs a nut tree and returns with a fistful of green almonds. George disappears with all Sevasti's girls and is found upstairs half an hour later teaching them the rumba. Katerina, paler than ever, surprises everyone by beginning to sing in a high, strong voice, beating time with a copper pan.

The priests have gone. The font has disappeared. The divers are showering *drachmae* on the men with the *bouzoukia*. A little longer, a little longer! Sevasti sloshes *retzina* mixed with paraffin with all the wild abandon of a maenad. Mikailis the *ferneze* dances alone and superbly, and a little woman in cracked boots cackles and joins him. She is marvellous. We clap and shout, and the room spins wildly.

We are all out on the dusty moonlit road, stumbling downhill through the piled rocks, past the flat pale cubes of the sleeping houses, following the *bouzoukia* home.

Even after two weeks of Carnival it was not easy to see or to say exactly what was happening. There had been nothing continuous, nothing organised … odd little spurts and jets of something … not Carnival, because the connotation of Carnival is gaiety and even in the dressing up of the children there had been nothing of gaiety. There were other things — grotesquerie, certain sly and sadistic touches of humour like little Georgouli's mockery of his mother, moments of a bizarre and sometimes frightening frenzy when the alleys spilled hordes of leaping, twirling, hopping little monsters into the dark evening pool of the *plateia*. But it didn't happen every night, and when it did happen it was never in the way nor at the time you expected. One night a youth ran the whole length of the waterfront, wearing only a lace curtain topped by an old German helmet — a lunatic figure, strange and inexplicable. For two nights afterwards all the children went back to playing five-stones and flying their kites, but in a sly and unnaturally subdued sort of way, as if they were only pretending to be normal.

It was not so much that something was happening, as that whatever was going to happen was imminent. An atmosphere of uneasy excitement simmered through the town, erupting into freakish invention and improvisation, dying down again. There was almost a weird sort of rhythm to it, a percussion rhythm, not music, for it was all barbaric. You caught the beat of it for a moment sometimes in the demented caperings of the children, and then you lost it again, as if the drummer had forgotten what he had set out to do and was just banging about idly, feeling for it, hoping to find it again.

During all this period the polite forms of greeting had changed. Instead of saying 'good morning' or 'good evening' you were greeted with *'Kaléss Apokriés!'* — good carnival. But it was all quite stiff and formal. There was no merriment in it. So far the dressing up, the masquerade, had been pretty much confined to the alley children. Yet even here 'dressing up' is the wrong phrase to use. They were not so much dressing up as *disguising* themselves, as if in their weird padding of rags and sheets and curtains and baskets, in their formlessness and facelessness, they could take themselves beyond humanity.

The two little stationers' shops were hung with festoons of paper hats and cheap cardboard devil masks printed in Athens, but there was not much sale for them. The children preferred to cover their faces completely with sheets or curtains or baskets, to obliterate identity altogether. If they wanted masks they made their own — hideous, leering bark or cardboard faces daubed with charcoal and red paint, related to jungle worlds far beyond the perimeters of Christianity.

Martin and Shane begged for hats and masks from the stationer's shop, and every evening they ran about the alleys with their friends. But their improvised costumes were always influenced by the memory of the fancy-dress parties or nursery charades of the wintry London afternoons. They were related to the tin trunk of 'dress-up things' and to Simon and Miranda and Matthew and Victoria Jane.

In the Kalymnian alleys, as in the London nurseries, they were identifying themselves with the characters of their imaginations. They were *being* somebody. They never achieved the horrible formlessness of their grotesquely disguised little friends, who were being nothing that has ever existed, except perhaps in the world of nightmare.

The Sunday marking the end of the second week of *Apokriés* took the whole population of the island to the inland village of Chorio for the dancing in the courtyard of the Church of the Virgin Mary. The young girls wore the traditional dress of Kalymnos, a straight, dignified tunic of dark striped silk slit at the sides and sleeves, with a wide brocaded sash tied at the back like a Japanese *obi* and one side of the skirt hooked up through the belt in a triangular flap like a large pocket to expose layers of beautifully hand-embroidered petticoats — a costume as striking and lovely as any I have seen. The women and girls who had no traditional costume improvised gipsy dresses with floral skirts and scarves, plastic aprons, and paper flowers behind their ears. Their faces were all painted in a crude and ghastly travesty of Western make-up (the Kalymnian woman normally does not even use lipstick) and their faces were covered with dozens of small spots of charcoal to simulate moles, which are greatly admired here. Even the prettiest looked scruffy and diseased.

The fact is that Kalymnian girls anyway don't make convincing gipsies. Even the little ones of twelve and thirteen are too grave, too circumspect in their actions. They know already, by imagination or experience, the weight of the responsibilities ahead of them.

Some of the young men had made themselves cowboy costumes — the cowboy as seen in the very old Western films shown at the Cinema Splendide has become something of a hero figure in Kalymnos — but it was significant that not one of the divers sacrificed his identity to the booted and spurred, gun-toting, Stetson-hatted heroism of the Wild West. The divers wore their own uniform of tight black trousers and peaked black caps, with a bright cummerbund wound around the waist and a coloured scarf twisted about the shoulders of their clean white shirts. All the men wore flowers tucked into their cap bands or behind their ears, red or white according to their romantic condition (red for passionate longing, white for fulfilment), and a few wore sprigs of green basil to mourn ostentatiously an unrequited love.

Retzina flowed, children grew fretful, mothers cross. Fathers disappeared into *tavernas*. Occasionally somebody would wander into the church to burn a candle to the Virgin. In the courtyard the crowd spun wilder and wilder circles and overflowed down the blue streets into houses and back yards, where other circles began to spin and spin ... around a single violin ... a clanging zither ... madly thrumming *bouzouki* ... a girl ecstatically singing ...

Led by singing priests, who in the power of their chanting and the determined set of their bearded faces seemed as if they might drive revelry from the town, a wedding party threaded its way through the twisting streets. The bride was a plump little girl of sixteen or so, still padded around the cheeks and throat with a child's puppy fat. The bridegroom was not much older. In their wax wreaths tied together with loops of white ribbon they looked pale and dazed and fearful and sacrificial. The wild music and the dancing that had spilled through the town had imparted a pagan flavour to the day. These two surely were the garlanded human offerings being led to the altar.

Under the fresh blue bowl of the spring sky the Carnival had finally achieved its form. The rhythm now was clear and definite and gay. And somehow it was anticlimactic. Whether it was that I had come to expect something different because of the running figure in the lace curtain and German helmet, or whether I was too sensitive to the dead and desolate towers of the abandoned Byzantine city that hung high and lonely and indifferent above the pretty streets, the embroidered petticoats, the paper roses, the ribboned *bouzoukia* ... at any rate that day of formal Carnival seemed less true to me than the antics of the alley children leading up to it. It was to prove much less true than the behaviour of the adults in the week that followed.

For as if the dancing at Chorio had provided some signal, some stimulus they had been awaiting, the adults took over the remaining week of Carnival.

Every night they wandered about the town in little bands — men padded lewdly with pillows and dressed as women, women hobbling in seamen's boots and scarecrow jackets. They drifted about the alleys silently, sometimes capering a little in the shadows, but always without a sound, sometimes swooping upon a passing pedestrian and making him the centre of a wild and soundless dance. Occasionally they would all rush together through lanes and houses and yards, up stairways and through lighted *tavernas*, beating bits of tin together or rattling gourds as they ran. It was seldom they made any noise like this, and when they did it was a little unnerving.

Often while we were eating our supper they would file quietly up the dark stairs and assemble around us in a silent circle. Their faces would be covered by hessian or sheeting with eye slits cut in it, or by baskets hung with fishnets and tassels. Around their waists they all wore girdles of dead, headless fish or the skeletons of fish, or a bunch of dried, queer-shaped gourds, or even saucepan lids. One figure was belted with strings of little dead birds hanging from their necks.

We never knew whether they were men or women, whether they were neighbours, friends or people we had never met. They never greeted us. They would caper and leap around the table quite silently. And then they would hit the saucepan lids with sticks and rattle the gourds in every corner of the room, and then they would bow and go out as quietly as they had come.

Angela and Maria could throw no light whatever on the custom. I think they were a little frightened by it, and they reacted rather irritably to inquiries.

'Ah, they're all potty here!' Maria said testily. 'Got no damned sense! They come in here, banging about and waking up the baby. Couldn't get Thoxouli to sleep for *hours* after! Fair screaming, she was. Honest, you'd think it was a pack of loonies let loose!'

'Did you chase them out?'

'Well ...' A pause and a rather sheepish grin. 'Well, you never know who they are, see, and I wouldn't want to offend nobody. Anyway, they're supposed to bring luck to your house. And God knows' — this with a sudden return to her normal asperity — 'we could do with a bit of it! Two babies squalling now instead of one. And both of them *girls*!'

Angela and Maria were making *Koliva* at the time. It was the second Soul Saturday; the third would come in the first week of Lent. One cannot help but wonder if there is not a closer connection between these Days for the Dead in midst of Carnival and the weird antics of the mummers than even the mummers themselves realise. Are the nightly visitors disguised so that prowling spirits will not recognise them? And the rattling gourds, the clashing saucepans — what else are they for if not to frighten desolate souls from the hearths of good people?

In Greek ceremony the pagan world is always there, lingering on, dark, impenitent, enigmatic, patient.

Later, on May Day, we saw it more clearly, when Sevasti roused us all long before dawn and led me off, stumbling and blinking with sleep, to fetch fresh water from the well. And when this was done she insisted that we all clamber up the damp, half-dark mountainside to see the sun shoot up — huge and jazzy orange — from a sea as white and thick and still as milk. There were hundreds of townspeople there already, the dawn watchers, rising up from the steaming stones on the mountain top, their arms filled with spiky flowers, their faces turned to the sun.

'Why, Sevasti? Why?'

'*Why?*' She looked at me in astonishment. 'Because this is what we do in Kalymnos. This is what we have always done.'

I let it go at that. Pondering drowsily upon Dionysian rites and fertility ceremonies from the days when the world was young, we filled our laps with flowers and, under Sevasti's instructions, plaited them into a large garland sharply bristling with spiky yellow blooms, and we took it down the mountainside and hung it over the door. Perhaps once, when the understanding of things was different, so great a mystery as the rising of the sun could not be taken for granted. It was necessary for the whole populace to reaffirm its faith in the daily miracle on a set occasion every year ... like examining one's safe deposit.

The wreath stayed on the door, wilted and sagging, until the feast of St John the Baptist seven weeks later, when the children took it down and cast it ceremoniously into Georgouli's bonfire. That evening there were fires burning all the way up the mountainside and through every street and lane in the town. And the valley as far back as Chorio was sprinkled with separate glowing points, like raked-over embers. Down every alley the children scurried beside their tall shadows marching on the walls, carrying old boxes, bundles of gorse, palm fronds, broken branches from the almond trees. Around every conflagration they strutted and danced, or leaped backwards and forwards through the flames, chanting gleefully, 'I leave my sins and my fleas behind me!'

It was, of course, the old pagan midsummer fire festival of purification dressed up in Christian guise and sanctified with a martyr's name.

Next morning everyone went down to the sea, even the very old grandmothers and the pregnant women, and with them they took their sheep and pigs and goats and hens, and they took little round sea pebbles called *tsalis*, blackened and still warm from the fires into which they had been thrown the night before. These were ceremoniously hurled out to sea, as far as they could be thrown. Then women, children, goats, sheep, pigs and all waded out from the shore and slowly submerged. It was a very curious spectacle.

The sea, of course, is an integral part of all Kalymnian ceremony. It is the ritual washing place for the sheets of the bridal couch, the sheets of the lying-in bed, the oil-and wine-soaked wrappings of the baptised child, the sheets from the bed of the dead. First fruits and last are offered to the sea. In Kalymnos his temples have gone, but Poseidon is still a mighty god. One ceases to wonder why so many of the boats in the harbour bear his name.

At Epiphany the bishop and all his attendant priests pay their homage to the sea, carrying the tiny silver cross from the cathedral down to the end of the quay in a beautiful and solemn ceremony. And then the cross of Christ is tossed far out into the cold winter harbour, where two score of naked and shivering young men will vie for the honour of diving for it and bringing it up triumphantly.

'Sea of the seamen, sea of mine,' begins the heartbreakingly beautiful Kalymnian song. 'Oh poor Kalymnos! You have blackened your mountains ...' And another says, 'I dream of your eyes because they are the colour of the sea, and the sea is always in my dreams ...' And yet another, 'Sea! Sea! Be as sugar, be as honey, for my love is sailing, winged like angels.' I know of no Kalymnian song that does not in some way make reference to the all-surrounding, impregnating sea.

In the last week of Carnival these were the songs we sang — the old songs, the songs of the sea, the true songs. They are songs filled with sadness, with winds and darkness and months of waiting, with lonely nights and young girls wearing black. I have seldom known anything more poignant than to hear them sung, deep and soft and sad, by a dozen jerseyed men who know what the songs mean and unselfconsciously invest each phrase with this private inward knowledge. Then the sea moves into the songs, surges in, the dark impetuous rush of it, its passion and poetry and loneliness, its cruelty and tenderness, and the men's own bitter thraldom to this oldest of mistresses.

We were singing on the last night of Carnival, still singing through the bewitched moonlit streets on our way to the house of Captain Miches, as we had sung at Skeftarios' until closing time. The mummers capered about us or touched us in silent greeting as they passed. The streets were curls of pale dust between the low flat squares of moon-pale houses, houses bleached out to the colour of sleep rising in insubstantial tiers to where the soft mountain shapes were smudged on the sky.

The house of Captain Miches seemed very beautiful, cut with open glowing squares of orange from windows and door, so that it was like a shell around an inner radiance. Inside it was clean and crowded, with a hospitable round table in the main room, a stiff settee with a snow-white embroidered cover and a sideboard piled with sponges and shells and *ikons*. In the corner was a big chromium-plated bed.

There were sixteen of us in the party, and it was almost midnight, but Miches' plump wife came sleepy and laughing to the door, her hair hanging down in two long black braids over a nightgown of pink flannel. She took the bottles and the lobsters and the fish that the divers thrust into her arms and spread a clean cloth across the table and began to set out the food. All the men moved about with an easy familiarity, finding chairs and lamps and extra plates and knives, and we could see Miches in the stone-floored kitchen chopping the lettuce for salad.

George and I, alone of all the party, were unfamiliar and a little formal in the glowing orange room. I felt with a sudden deep conviction that we had no right to be there. This was something that belonged to the men in black caps, to great ugly Miches and to his plump and pigtailed wife, to Fotes and Costas Manglis and to handsome Mikailis, the *colazáris*. George must have felt exactly the same thing, for he made a sudden surprising little speech, apologising for our intrusion at such a late hour.

'*What!*' Miches' wife paused round-eyed, a plate of lobster claws stiffly extended over the white tablecloth. 'What is this? Miches, do you hear what they say, our guests?'

Miches winked at us and grabbed her around the wide, firm waist. Nightgown, braids of hair, lobster claws and all went spinning and waltzing around the laden table.

'Every night!' she gasped. 'Every night like this!' She protested pinkly as she spun, and she was so round and flushed in the lamplight, so warm still with sleep and the certainty of those two huge encircling arms that I knew it would never matter at what time Miches came home, nor how many guests he brought with him. All too soon now the lamplit room would be empty, and for seven long months she would start up in vain in the chromium bed in that tidy room, listening for the lurching footsteps and the deep-bayed chorus surging up the alley.

Handsome Mikailis the *colazáris*, who lived in the house next door, reappeared, herding before him two shamefaced girls wrapped in long dressing-gowns of brightly patterned cotton. They looked children. One was Mikailis' wife, the other her sister.

'Just the job! Just the job!' Mikailis yelled, using his only English words like a muleteer's cry as he prodded the girls into the crowded room. They fled for the bed, curling themselves into the corner with their feet tucked under their dressing-gowns and their eyes obstinately lowered. Miches' wife kissed them both and then everybody, including Mikailis, ignored them completely, although every now and then he would toss a lobster claw to them over his shoulder. They would pick at it delicately, whispering together. Occasionally I would look up to see four huge dark eyes fixed on me unblinkingly, but when I smiled the eyelids would come down like black-fringed blinds and both girls would be absorbed in tracing the patterns on their dressing gowns.

An hour or two had passed, I suppose, and the nine lobsters were a mountain of scarlet debris on the table, when Mikailis rose with a shouted, 'Oop-la!' and turned to the girls. 'Go on, you get up and sing for us,' he commanded. And, surprisingly enough, they did. Without giggles or whispers, with no trace of nervousness or self-consciousness, they stood in the corner of the room, holding their dressing gowns around them. And they opened their soft young throats and sang. It was inevitably of the sea they sang, of the men sailing away and the women waiting, and they sang in the sweet, clear, effortless voices of children.

Mikailis' wife, the taller of the two, was just sixteen, Miches told me. She had been married for a year. Her sister was fourteen and would marry during the next winter, when she reached her fifteenth birthday. They were as fresh and lovely as flowers, or soft-breasted singing birds. And like birds they sang, without thought or care, the songs they were born to sing, the heartbreaking songs of Kalymnian women.

Even Fotes was silent when they had done, and Miches' wife was sitting very straight on the bed, staring at the shadowed wall with wet black eyes.

'Just the job, eh?' Mikailis said, but he said it in a puzzled sort of way, and the playful punch he aimed at Fotes' ear was half-hearted.

It was no more than a continuation of the spell when the front door opened quietly and the group of mummers stepped noiselessly into the smoky orange room, bringing a breath of the night with them, the warm, waning night that barely had the strength to flicker the lamp flames.

Their shadows swooped and plunged on the wall, dancing blackly above the blind white faces, the leering masks, the bizarre hunched shapes spinning and lunging in a ring around the table. And at the table the strong, dark, hard men sat like little children, trustful, with still hands and wondering brown eyes. And in the corner of the room the three women stood together in their long gowns and braided hair, as though they might at any moment burst forth, all together, with another new, triumphant song.

14

At some time in the long vacuum of Lent we finished the novel. Emptied at last of the energy and effort we had summoned and expended day by day and week by week for so many months, we were left with those gaping hollows of purposelessness which seem to be the natural seepage tanks for all the sly frets and fears which can only be kept dammed up by work.

In the urgency of our progress towards this goal we had seldom thought beyond it. To get the book done, that was the first thing; and sometimes even the goal itself had receded mistily beyond the immediate problems and excitements of the story and the people who possessed us more entirely than we realised. If we ever did pause to consider what would come after, it was to tell ourselves hastily that we were working hard and could do nothing beyond that to secure the future we wanted.

Now that the work was done and the bulky package of typewritten sheets parcelled and posted we came to realise that the future had been out of our hands from the moment we crossed our fingers and shoved the package through the hinged slot in the blue box. It was for somebody else now to decide whether we could go on living in Greece.

The whistling in the dark which had characterised our earlier uncertainties would no longer do. We were afflicted with a pervasive melancholy which seemed to tinge everything around us with the presage of parting and loss. We found ourselves being unusually attentive to what was said even in the idlest conversation, lest we miss some fragment to be remembered, some phrase of accidental poetry. We would stop for a long time by a woman weaving in a doorway, beside a group of children flying their kites, a girl filling a jar at the well, the glistening mounds of aubergines in the market. We would sit on the balcony in the evening to watch the people walking and the light changing on the mountain slopes and the shepherds climbing the darkening zigzag trail to Vathy and the distant shape of Kos below the evening star. It was as if we were both aware of a desperate need to store and hoard each separate coloured fragment of this strange loved little world against the day when it would no longer be ours.

In this mood we were less surprised than we might otherwise have been when Yanni came one day to inform us that his uncle Manolis had finally been persuaded to return to his family on Kos. With diminishing hope we had been working towards this objective for two months, but we had never really believed that the objective might be achieved. Indeed the ascending evening step on the stairs, the shabby, stooped figure in the doorway, the apologetic murmur, 'Good evening, my dear brother and my sister,' we had come to accept as natural and inevitable, like the cockroaches in the kitchen or the way the toilet choked when the wind drove the sea in from the south or the midnight blare of *bouzoukia* music from the row of coffee-houses. It was an irritation the very familiarity of which had long since blunted all but a dull, persistent sense of discomfort. If Manolis had not arrived by the time we were ready to eat, I would automatically set aside a portion for him to have later. I would grumble as I did so, but I would always do it.

'Excuse me for speaking, but you shouldn't do that,' Yanni had said to me once.

'Why not?'

'Because every evening my uncle eats first at the home of my brother Mikailis, and then comes here to eat again.'

'He *what!*'

'Sometimes he eats also at the home of his sister Calliope, then with Mikailis, then with you. Three times he eats. Why do you think Mikailis doesn't visit you any more? Because he is ashamed to sit and watch my uncle eating all your food when his belly is already full.'

It was true that the soft step of Mikailis had not followed that of Manolis up the stairs for some weeks, but this had been such a relief in the sheer weight of the nightly invasion that we had scarcely noticed it. Yanni, on the other hand, was always there. Sometimes, with mock deference, he followed his uncle up the stairs; sometimes he came first so that he could settle himself into the easy chair which Manolis had come to regard as his own. Manolis' outrage at the usurpation of his privileges by a mere nephew gave Yanni a great sense of satisfaction. ('He has a free heart, that Yanni,' Leonidas the cake seller once said of him, 'and a tongue like an eel!')

Usually George would be hunched over the manuscript at the end of the long table, pretending to read or make corrections, swearing, as he swore every night, that he would sit them out if they stayed till dawn. But there was no way of sitting them out. They had the patience of their race and they were as firmly rooted as ancient temples. George's rage or sullenness or frigidity passed completely over their heads. They could not be frozen off; they seemed oblivious of tension or atmosphere. They simply waited in Sphinx-like silence until we capitulated and led them off to a *taverna*, with Yanni whistling gaily to himself, Manolis hunching along in the rear like a sulky child and George suffering severely from his nervous dyspepsia.

It had happened like this every night for four months.

Now the story which Manolis had told us was that the Kalymnian tailor for whom he worked owed him six weeks' wages, and he dared not go back to Kos for fear that it would never be paid. The paltry few *drachmae* he did get each week, he said, had to be sent to Kos to support his wife and children. His accounts of the poverty of his family were deeply harrowing. His little boy, almost blind from malnutrition, had eaten snails from the garden fence because there was nothing else to eat. His mother had wept all that night, praying for a miracle. And the next morning the fifty-*drachmae* note which George had given him (the first, incidentally, of a steady supply) had arrived, and the whole family had gone to church to light candles and pray for blessings to fall upon their saviour. Occasionally Manolis went across to Kos for a weekend visit. There would be more fifty-*drachmae* notes from George, who would also pay the boat fare and provide baskets of tinned food and butter and milk and clothing for the children and little surprise packets of toys and coloured pencils and sweets. In some respects Manolis had become our most costly luxury.

Later inquiries — less inquiries than scraps of gossip and information filtering to our ears — revealed that the old rogue had been telling us a fine old pack of lies from the very beginning. Not only had he been paid regularly by the tailor, but he had been paid a good deal more than either of his nephews earned, and they, with our assistance, had been supporting him for all these months! Moreover, while he was living in some comfort on Kalymnos his wife and family on Kos were being supported by his father-in-law, a market gardener in fairly good circumstances. It was no wonder that Manolis clung to Kalymnos!

'We've got to put a stop to it,' George said.

'How?'

'He'll have to be persuaded to go back to Kos and stay there.'

'Yes, but how?'

'Do what Yanni said. Stop feeding the old bastard!'

It was hard to do, but we were desperate. We would take our evening meal very early, with the children, so that by the time Manolis arrived the table would be cleared, the dishes washed and stacked away. We would be very busy with our books and papers.

Yanni would be sitting in the corner, grinning and whistling and humming to himself or making pointed remarks about Lent and the necessity for fasting. In the end it was the fast that gave us our solution.

In the homes of both Yanni and his brother Mikailis there was strict fasting. Not so much as a drop of oil or a blob of margarine found its way into the plain macaroni or rice. There were no meat, fish, eggs, cheese or anything of animal origin. The women of Kalymnos are among the most pious of all Greeks, and I honestly think it gave them a real sense of satisfaction to feel their bones beginning to poke through their wasting flesh and their cheeks to sink in. I felt sorriest for the children, who were forced to observe the long fast also. The men, of course, were perfectly all right. In their houses they scrupulously observed the fast — and made up for it the moment they got down to the *plateia* or into one of the *tavernas*. Golden Anna cooked more meat and egg dishes through Lent than at any other time of the year.

'After all,' the men would explain, 'I am a working man. I cannot drag that *carro* (or hammer up that balcony or haul in that net) with nothing in my guts. I do not wish to be deceitful, but this is the way of it. The Lord will understand. It is only that I am just as sure that Irini (or Polymnea or Xanthippe) will not. It's a terrible thing that a man should lie just in order to fill his belly. But there you are.'

Now all this placed Manolis in a very invidious position. In the houses of his relatives he could now get nothing but the most austere Lenten foods and on the more severe fast days he could get nothing whatever, not even a crust of dry bread. And as it was more than he could bear that he should spend a *drachma* on food, he hurried to us faster than ever, knowing that our diet had not changed.

It was an agony having to watch him shift around on his chair as the evening wore on and I still made no move towards the kitchen. I had never seen him looking so thin, so shabby, so miserably pathetic. It was pitiful to see his sunken eyes, the flesh sagging under the grey stubble on his cheeks, the one great yellow tooth jiggling between the downward hook of his mottled nose and the upward thrust of his chin.

'My dear brother and sister,' he would say at last, 'do you not go out tonight? I heard that Skeftarios bought some fine *barbunia* in the market this morning. If you have not already had your food ...'

And George would look up from his papers with unrelenting eyes and say mildly, 'Well, you know how it is, Manolis. We don't get out much in Lent. We wouldn't want to offend the people who feel strongly about that sort of thing.'

Gradually we wore him down, and then Yanni brought us the tidings that Manolis had decided at last to return to his family. There was work for him with a Koan tailor for the rest of the winter, and when summer came he would take up his old job with the municipality, spraying the wells and springs and drinking places to keep down mosquitoes.

'Oh lord!' George said, suddenly contrite. 'The poor old bastard. I suppose we were responsible for bringing him here in the first place. You can't altogether blame him for making the most of it. I think I'll give him a couple of hundred *drachmae* ... soften the blow a little.'

We saw him off on the little *Angellico,* the same caique that had brought us on that stormy wintry day, with Manolis stepping ashore like a king returning from exile. *'My dear brother and sister, I bring you now to Kalymnos ...!'*

'Well, Manolis, it'll be better for you to be with your wife and children again,' we said half-heartedly, feeling like monsters at the sight of the tears seeping from his wrinkled eyes. After all, with all his iniquities, the old rogue loved us truly. And this was another ending. I was glad of the stiff, crackling envelope sticking out of his top pocket, glad of the basket of food and clothing and toys and chocolate we hoisted on board after him. And Yanni and Mikailis had brought their parting gifts too — cigarettes and eggs and a trussed hen in a netting bag. We all stayed to wave until the *Angellico* had rounded the breakwater and was out of sight.

'Eeeeh! Now let's all go to Skeftarios' tonight!' Mikailis, whom we had scarcely seen for weeks, was rubbing his hands together joyfully and skipping about on his small, dainty feet. Yanni was yelping like a small boy let out of school. And we were so weak with relief that we agreed without demur, quite forgetting that on our first night of freedom we had promised ourselves a walk, just the two of us, to Lavassi. But all the family are like that. They catch you off guard. And before you know it you've committed yourself again.

None of us felt really well next morning. At midday, when the *Angellico* came back from Kos, I was still mooning ineffectually around the window. I could hear George rustling around with papers in the children's room. Yanni was coming across the *plateia*, heading for the house, and somehow it was a relief to see that he too appeared as sick and doleful as we were.

'How is Mikailis? Does he feel bad too?'

'He isn't so well.' Yanni sighed heavily. 'I met him just now coming from the pier.' He studied the ends of his fingers. 'You know the *Angellico* is in?'

'I saw it, yes.'

'Did you see who was on it?'

'Not —' George was leaning weakly against the door frame.

'Yes,' said Yanni, and then we heard the old familiar step on the stairs.

'Ah, my dear brother and sister,' said Manolis as he walked into the room.

15

Here they still call Easter *Lambri*, with the accent hard on the final syllable, from the name of a tiny spotted insect which at this time of the year clouds every mountain stone. Only the educated and pedantic say *Pasca*.

For all Greeks it is the most important of the year's festivals. In the absolutely pure form in which it is observed on Kalymnos one sees a ceremony which for true drama and moving sincerity would be hard to rival.

In the beginning Easter was calculated to coincide with the Jewish Passover, falling on the fourteenth day after the vernal equinox. At the Council of Nicea, called by Constantine the Great in 325, it was decided that Easter must always be celebrated on a Sunday. The learned scholars of Alexandria, then the centre of the scientific world, would fix the date. According to the Julian calendar then in use the vernal equinox occurred on April 3rd. With Pope Gregory's reform of the calendar in 1582 this date was changed to March 21st. Today, although the Gregorian calendar is used in Greece, the Orthodox Church continues to use the old Julian date as the basis for its calculations. Thus Greek Easter never falls before April 3rd and often varies as much as five weeks from the Easter observance of other European churches.

For the Kalymnians the festival has a significance even apart from its deep religious implications. Easter marks the end of the long winter idleness. As soon as the six-day festival is over the sponge fleet sails for Africa.

In the last week of Lent most of the diving boats had come back freshly painted and rigged from the Lavassi shipyard. Beneath our window they tossed in rank upon coloured rank, spangled in sunlight, with a forest of little flags snapping over them in the fresh, bright wind. The big two-masted *depositos*, great high-powered lumps of ships like medieval caravels, were moored along the breakwater pier running out to the lighthouse. Six or seven of them were still beached on the shingle behind the Customs House, with gangs of men burning off and caulking and painting all day long. Other men were swinging from the thick pine masts, reeving the new rope, stiff and white, through gaily coloured blocks carved to simulate fish and aeroplanes and sea birds, or tarring down the standing rigging.

During the week the farmers had come down too, wearing their wide flat hats secured beneath their chins with leather thongs and their soft goatskin knee boots. They had come from the mountains above Vathy and Piso and Chorio and Argos to bring the Pascal lambs to the town. All that week the *plateia* was filled with Easter lambs, delicate, crinkled creatures still awkward on their thin legs. Their soft fleeces were dyed rose pink and crimson and yellow and blue and green. Around their throats they had garlands of flowers or woven ropes of brightly coloured wool supporting bundles of multi-coloured woollen balls that the children had spent weeks in making.

Looking down from the balcony it seemed as if the vivid waves of boats must have burst across the *plateia* in the night and soughed away again, leaving blobs and clots of coloured froth behind.

The whole tempo of the town had changed. Every day in Holy Week the bells of all the campaniles rang for service after service, and there was not a church on the island that was not packed with emaciated women, fanatical in this final week of fasting, almost beside themselves with a mounting sense of tension and excitement. One could not help admiring their fervour and fortitude, to say nothing of their willpower, for while they starved, the whole island was heavy with the smell of food cooking.

It had begun on the Saturday before with the baking of the Lazarus bread for the Feast of the Raising of Lazarus, a festival, like that of John the Baptist, of particular significance to Greek Orthodox. The little loaves of sweet Lazarus bread were beautifully modelled, with a formalised body in a winding sheet, folded hands and stiff thick legs with crudely indicated toes. The best of them looked as if Epstein might have made them.

The festival of Lazarus was a joyful day for all the children, who would go singing from door to door asking for dyed eggs or money. (Shane and Martin memorised the Lazarus song the day before and set off with a wire basket early in the morning. They did not return until nightfall. Their take had been seventeen eggs and eleven *drachmae*, but unfortunately the eggs were all scrambled on the pavement during an altercation with a rival party!)

During the week that followed, hundreds of thousands of eggs must have been dyed — mostly red, but sometimes blue — and ovens were busy all day making *koulouria* (small sweet pastries twisted into shapes of flowers and baskets and serpents) or stylised cradles with a red egg for the baby's head, and the great cartwheel loaves of sesame-scented Easter bread brushed with beaten egg and stamped with mystical symbols.

The bakehouses were hard put to cope with it all. Not only were the ovens crowded with the endless trays of *koulouria* and *aphgoulis* and the huge wheels of Easter bread, but all the furnaces were still busy night and day baking the tens of thousands of hard little *galetis* — exactly like the old seabiscuits or hardtack of windjammer days — which would sustain the divers during their long summer at sea. Fotes brought a couple to the house for us to taste. 'Not bad,' I said, once I had bitten into one without losing any teeth. 'I like it.'

'Sure,' said Fotes dryly. 'So do the weevils.'

Mikailis and the other labourers were busier now than they had been all the year or would be again. The loading of the boats with big sacks of *galetis* and flour and macaroni and rice and drums of petrol and oil and water was a big job, because a great many chartered boats had come in from the other islands — from Hydra and Symi and Samos and Rhodes, from Leros and Kos and Astypalaia, and even from Piraeus and New Phaleron — and with the big Kalymnian fleet already assembled there were about a hundred and fifty boats ready to sail off for the African spongebeds.

The actual diving gear was never handled by anyone but the divers themselves. All day now they moved backwards and forwards across the *plateia*, threading their way through farmers and flocks of multi-coloured sheep and children staggering about with lambs in their arms and starved women running from the bakehouse with great trays of pastries and bread on their heads.

We could see them all from the balcony — Fotes and Saklarades and Costas and Miches and Mikailis and young Captain Charlie and all the others, loaded with coils of new rubber hosing and copper helmets and weighted boots and the carefully patched and tested rubber suits of the *skafendros* and the lightweight black suits of the *ferneze* divers.

At night it was even more exciting, for in every back street and vacant lot big charcoal fires were burning and women were holding lanterns to light the huge iron cauldrons in which the salted beef was stewing. The women lend only light and companionship to the work. It is the men who do the cooking. We would see them squatting around the cauldrons, stirring every now and then with the thick billet of wood, tasting occasionally, sniffing speculatively at the rich smell. What would it taste like five or six months from now? Saklarades tells us, in one lugubrious word that sets all the divers laughing until the tears course down their cheeks and must be wiped away with the backs of their hands.

It is Saklarades who insists that we take an *oka* or two so that the children can have a 'real sponge diver's meal' of boiled salt beef and *galetis*. (Martin and Shane, eyes stretched wide and jaws aching and faces agonised with the salt, chew their way through to the last shred and inform us that they feel very strong indeed after such a fine meal. They are torn now between the desire to hang around the boats and the divers and the desire to spend all day on the mountainside with the children who are grazing their coloured lambs.)

Sevasti is now so weak and thin with fasting that she can no longer carry the water jars, and one of her girls comes with her every morning to do the heavier work. Yanni has long wranglings with her in the kitchen on the folly of starvation. He has no more success than we. She will eat on Sunday morning, when Christ has risen. Yanni's own wife is in much the same plight but, as he points out, she has far greater reserves of flesh. He brings his children often to the house while his wife is at church and we feed them bread and butter and jam and eggs and milk. They promise not to tell their mother, and they are made to wash carefully around their mouths before they go home.

Wednesday is the day set aside for the blessing of the boats and this year the bishop himself is to give his benediction to the sponge fleet. The *Saint George*, a fine-looking white boat with a lime-green trim, one of a diving unit of four, has been chosen as the representative boat.

On the after deckhouse the divers have improvised a pretty little altar with an embroidered cloth, a handful of fresh flowers and two tall candlesticks borrowed from the church of Saint Stephanos. From the starboard stays flies the great tasselled banner of the saint himself, a rich and wonderful flag of old cream silk and satin embroidered with silver and gold. The picture of Saint Stephanos, thin and ascetic, sways in a queer stylised dance above the earnest faces of the men. The old miraculous *ikon* has also been brought from the church and propped up on the deckhouse. It is a magnificent *ikon*: the hands and halo are of hammered gold and the painting beneath the silver casing is very old, painted with power and dignity. From the bottom of the frame hang scores of divers' amulets, little silver cut-out boats and diving helmets and figures of divers, a scrap of sponge tied to a piece of string, a tiny ship in a tiny bottle, even a shark's tooth and the dried tip of an octopus tentacle.

The bishop arrives with eight attendant priests, all clad in their most brilliant robes, led, surprisingly, by Dimitri the cigarette boy and two of his street-urchin friends, almost unrecognisable in white and blue satin and with improbably scrubbed faces. One after another the priests climb aboard, holding up their long skirts as they negotiate the narrow, swaying plank. Again I have a faint sense of shock and incongruity at the sight of the well-pressed trousers and the pointed, polished shoes under robes so richly Byzantine and so magnificently coloured. Suddenly they all seem dressed up, and one of them, I notice, has a hole in his sock.

Nevertheless, the service is most moving, sung full and loud on the scrubbed deck planks, with the rich ripple of fine silks moving against the improvised altar and the now white rigging moving against the crisp spring sky. The bareheaded men in the little band seem smaller and paler than usual with their shaven jaws and slicked-down hair and clean white collars buttoned under jackets that have been brushed and pressed.

One of the divers holds the enamelled basin of holy water as the bishop goes around blessing every part of the boat. He is very thorough, clambering over the equipment with his purple robe hooked up around his hips, negotiating the piled stores and coils of rope with the ease of long practice. He dips his sprig of mountain herbs into the basin as he goes, sprinkling everything he sees. The men are blessed, and the sea around them, and the rudder and the wheel and the diving ladder and the anchor bitts and the drums of food, the engine, tiller, ropes, airlines, rubber diving suits, anchors, the primitive little brazier that will cook the food, the stanchions and scuppers — everything, he blesses.

And when it is all done he takes the basin from the diver and empties all the holy water that is left into an upturned diving helmet. It is a warm, spontaneous gesture, and the divers laugh suddenly and rush forward to kiss his hand.

(After such a very colourful and comprehensive blessing it seemed unjust that the *Saint George* should go into the cliffs and sink the following week during a test run to the north side of the island! Captain Miches entirely blamed Stephanos, the owner of the boat, for having allowed the bishop to bless it. The bishop, explained Miches, was the best of men and deservedly popular, but he was just no good for boats. With women and children he was wonderful, and brought them all the luck in the world, but with boats … he shook his head solemnly. 'No good!' he said. His final ruling on the matter was that Stephanos should have known better.)

On the night of Maundy Thursday the true religious ecstasy begins to take over the town. Every church is packed and children fill the streets and lanes outside. We choose the big and rather ugly church of Saint Nicholas because we are a big party. Angela, recovered and purified, is able to come, and with her Maria and little Thoxouli, and all the men, women and children of half a dozen neighbouring families.

The church is just as ugly within as without, but tonight the singing is magnificent. The Greek Orthodox service is primarily composed of singing — almost a primitive form of oratorio using four separate singing groups; the priests, two choirs facing each other across the body of the church from high rostra, and the congregation itself. Within this framework of a musical form, together with the highly formalised and extremely dramatic acting of the story to be told, the service as it progresses acquires a sombre magnificence that is more akin to the smouldering Byzantine icons hanging in the darkness of the altar screen than to the cheap marble and tawdry mid-Victorian religious paintings that disfigure the body of the church.

If you were to seek even an approximate parallel to this service in England — and it would have to be very approximate indeed — you might glimpse it in the performance of the medieval mystery plays in York Minster. You would never find it in any established Western church ceremony.

The singing itself remains purely Byzantine, based on the traditional monodic form — the voices, that is, singing in unison but not in harmony. (Instrumental music of any sort is forbidden. Only the human voice is considered worthy to utter praise of the Lord.) There is no fixed rhythm or regular division into measures, the stress coming entirely according to the accent of the word. A further complication to an ear attuned to Western music is the fact that the Byzantine scale instead of having two modes, a major and a minor, has eight. Modifications, of course, have been unavoidable down the centuries (the last official modification was made some three centuries ago, but even today there are a dozen schools of thought in Athens on the way Byzantine music should properly be sung) and the Turkish and Arabic influences show clearly in the music.

Services are almost always very long, usually lasting from three to six hours and even on special occasions running all through the night.

Tonight the priests and choirs are to sing twelve bibles, or portions of the Gospel. After the singing of the fifth Christ is brought out on His cross and taken in sad, solemn, candlelit procession around the church. The figure is cut out of cardboard and rather crudely painted, with a silk cloth draped around its loins and a wreath of mountain thorns on its head.

The effect as the rather shabby and cheap-looking effigy is placed upright in the centre of the nave is quite electric. Women, sobbing uncontrollably, cast themselves to the floor, wringing their hands and clutching their hair. Children wail and men cover their eyes. It is all completely sincere and deeply moving. To these people the Crucifixion is not something read about in a book or explained by a curate over a plate of thin cucumber sandwiches. It is *now* that Christ is dying on the cross, as he will be dying *now*, on this night, forever. That is why most of the women will stay in the church all night, shivering on the marble floor, to mourn beside the cross.

From Sevasti's ghastly haggard face on Good Friday morning I know that she had been prostrate all night before the cross in the church of Agios Mummas, where she usually worships. Her eyes are bloodshot, her hands trembling.

Good Friday is a complete fast. On this day even the men will not eat more than a handful of olives. In the afternoon the whole population goes from church to church to inspect the various *Epitáphios* which the women have prepared to symbolise the fact that Christ has been taken from the cross and placed in his tomb.

These funeral biers are incredibly lovely, roofed with little domes of silver or blue enamel, hung with silver gauze and white satin, with wreaths of flowers and tinsel bows. One is covered all over with handmade flowers of white organdy, thousands of them. Another has gauze curtains worked entirely with silver beads. Some have candles at the corners. And the more ambitious devise ingenious systems of lighting. There is a carpet before each bier, flanked by tubs of mint and flowers, and the bare cross is also wreathed with flowers. Little cardboard cutouts of the Marys mourn at each side of the bier.

The churches have been taken over absolutely by the women — one is close again to the beginnings — and everywhere there are dark, still figures massed about the crosses. It is the women who weep, the women who mourn, the women who sew the winding sheet.

Nevertheless they are still women, and one is expected to praise their handiwork lavishly and to disparage slightly the *Epitáphios* of the other churches.

As the day wears on it develops into rather a jolly social occasion. We meet all our friends, strangely *en famille* today and all dressed in their very best. We drink innumerable cups of coffee and tiny glasses of *mastika* and *strega*. We must have walked six miles from church to church by the time we find ourselves back on the *plateia* buying pretty paper lanterns for the children to take on the evening procession. They are too excited to eat, and they are put to bed in their clothes with the promise that they will be awakened the moment the procession begins.

At nine o'clock we hear the chanting. Out on the dark *plateia* we can see hundreds of points of candle flame and the bobbing orange glow of lanterns. Within five minutes the processions from all the other churches have poured down the lanes and mountainsides like rivers of flame, and in the street there are thousands of candles winking on the gold and the silver of the crosses and shields borne by the altar boys. Singing women and girls holding tall candles are massed about the biers borne shoulder high by relays of men.

From our balcony the scene is mysterious and magnificent — the glittering white biers lurching high above the flickering points of flame, like nuptial howdahs borne by invisible elephants. The whole *plateia* brims with the solemn chant — the deep tones of the men, the strained, sobbing voices of the women, the high piping of the children. Around the *Epitáphios* of Agios Christos are the slow throb of drums and the rich purples and reds and yellows of the ceremonial robes of the bearded priests. The bishop wears a crown of gold wire studded with coloured glass and a cloak of purple satin made in the form of many heavy overlapping fans.

He is, as always, an impressive figure, but I am moved most deeply by the dark massings and groupings of the singing women with the candlelight flickering on their taut, pale, exhausted faces, and by the sudden blazings of gold high in the darkness above the swaying biers, where the tall swinging lanterns burn on tasselled shields and raised crosses. There are the bobbing Chinese lanterns of the children, little blobs of orange light jumping almost at ground level. Faces swim out of the crowd, suddenly illuminated ... closed eyes, straining throats, mouths stretched wide in ecstasy. And very high, high on the dark shape of the mountain against the stars, is a ridge of dancing points of flame. The nuns of Agios Pandas have brought out their candles to the great rock that overhangs the town.

Emotion still grips the whole town on Saturday morning. In every lane and doorway the little coloured lambs the children have loved and tended all the week are being ritually slaughtered. Crosses are being smeared above every doorway with the running blood from their throats. It is too much. I cannot bring myself to move out of the house all morning, not until the butchery is over and the streets are clean again.

By midday the lambs are going to the furnaces, curled in the traditional Easter pots of red earthenware patterned with curious white symbols. (The symbols look more pagan than Christian, but nobody seems to understand the meaning of them.) The lambs are stuffed with rice and liver and cinnamon, the air heavy with the smell of blood and spices and cooking.

After sundown the *tavernas*, which have been closed all day, are permitted to open, and the men flock to them. 'What time does Christ rise?' The people ask the question in the same matter-of-fact tone that they would use if asking what time the shops opened or a ship was leaving.

At exactly ten o'clock the bells begin to ring — Christos first, then Nicholas, the urgent clamour of I-papandi and the throaty clangour of Saint Stephanos on the hill, Mummas in the glen. And all the churches take it up along the dark valley … the night is wild with bells.

Tonight we follow the largest crowd to the cathedral. The children carry tall white candles decorated with flowers. Their pockets are stuffed with red eggs and *koulouria* and lethal-looking home-made fireworks.

A wooden platform decorated with palm leaves has been set up in the courtyard outside the church. Inside there is not even standing room. The atmosphere is now joyous and expectant. Everybody sings, and there is no sobbing, although the older women in the upper gallery look just about at their last gasp. Just before midnight the chandeliers are doused, and all the tall candles. Only faint illumination comes from the little oil lamp that burns perpetually before the icon of Christ on the high altar.

If it were not for that tiny glow it would be the darkness of the tomb — which is what it is meant to simulate.

Suddenly, with a sense of dramatic timing that any professional actor might envy, the bishop appears before the altar holding a long lighted taper aloft and crying, 'Come ye and take light from the eternal light!'

There is a wild surge forward into the darkness, a tumult of gasping, pressing bodies, a sea of upraised hands holding candles. One by one their tapers take light from his, or from one another's and the flickering pinpoints spread and multiply through the gloom until all the church is bathed in the flickering radiance. On the tossing, flame-pricked tide we are borne along, willy-nilly, in the procession that follows the bishop from the church.

Now on the palm-wreathed platform under the open starry sky they are singing of Mary and the Magdalene at the tomb, and of the stone rolled away. And at exactly midnight the Angel cries:

'He is not here! He is risen!' From the churches of Nicholas and Stephanos great explosions like cannonfire shake the night, and all of us outside the cathedral are caught in a great wild bombardment of red eggs and those terrible home-made fireworks.

Children, completely out of control with all this pent-up drama and unleashed hysteria, are whacking each other with eggs, stuffing their mouths with *koulouria* and hurling fireworks like the very little fiends of hell. We fight our way home as through a battlefield under heavy fire.

'Christ is risen!'

'He is risen indeed!'

'Christ is risen!'

A procession from Saint Nicholas is snaking up the mountain with little bobbing lanterns. Going where?

All through the night the parties continue, for the great fast is over and there are red eggs and Easter bread and *koulouria* and sweet black wine and a special stew made from the visceral organs of the slaughtered lamb.

On every hand invitations are extended to us to come and eat — 'Come and eat! Christ is risen! Eat with us!' — but it has all been too much, and we decline the invitations courteously and go home to bed. Things go whoomp all through the night.

On Sunday, however, we can no longer avoid or evade their hospitality. Twenty families send dishes of the choicest morsels of the wonderful Easter lamb-and-rice dish around to our house. We have enough *koulouria* and loaves of Easter bread and red eggs to stand a month's siege. We eat until our bellies are like drums.

Through the stuffed stupor of that day I remember Sevasti's girls coming to inform me that she is ill. Who can wonder, with that sort of food in that quantity after forty days of near starvation!

Sunday — and a Greek Easter — draws to its close in a ghastly symphony of snores and retching. Only the very pious are capable of waddling to church. We are not.

'Christ is risen!' shouts a drunken, reeling group of divers beneath our windows. They emphasise this indisputable truth by bombarding our door with fireworks that sound like hand grenades.

'He is risen indeed!' we respond politely, and close the shutters.

16

'Well ... well, good-bye,' Fotes said. He shook hands somewhat embarrassedly over the bowed and sobbing head of his wife. Her tired, toothless face was bruised a little and swollen, but whether from weeping or from the beating it was rumoured Fotes had inflicted on her as a finale to his week of drunkenness it was not for us to say. Neither was it for an outsider to say whether her weeping indicated a real grief that Fotes was going away or merely a tired relief at the prospect of having her housekeeping money paid regularly through the bank for the next seven months, and peace in her house. To the wives of so many of the divers, that recuperative period after the winter revelries must be of immense importance.

Across her shoulder Fotes' shaky, white-lipped, half-apologetic grimace said, *women!* He looked terribly sick.

Along the stone quay, among the blanket rolls, the checked gingham bundles, the baskets covered with clean white cloths sewed down very tightly with neat stitches, the weeping women, the excited children, the flagons of *retzina* and the bottles of *ouzo*, all the divers who were to leave that day stood awkwardly and unaccustomedly in their family groups — some with a comforting arm around their women, some nursing the youngest or the most importunate of their many clamouring children, some, still drunk, propped upright by brothers or cousins or the more sober among their friends, or held in a roughly vertical position only by the pressure of the women clinging to them.

The day before, when Saklarades' boat had been scheduled to sail, a search party had been out for two hours scouring all the *tavernas* in the port and out through Chorio as far as Brosta before the divers had been rounded up, Saklarades among them, bellowing like a bull, his great upraised fist battering most joyfully.

Dimitri the cigarette boy, turned ferryman this afternoon with his uncle's dinghy, was singing as he manoeuvred in towards the quay steps to pick up the next load.

Between the pier and the high rocky crags, where the houses clung around the black dome of Saint Stephanos like snippets of the sky pasted on, ten diving boats — five of them white and five of them crimson — quilted a ruched and intricate pattern on the dull silk spread of the afternoon harbour. The two big mother ships accompanying the little flotilla were anchored out beyond the lighthouse. They sat wide and heavy into the sea, swinging slowly and sluggishly on their anchor chains while the diving boats skimmed and circled lightly around them in a dance as brilliant and tireless as the summer ecstasies of a swarm of dragonflies.

Good-bye … good-bye … Fotes and Costas Manglis in the sternsheets of the dinghy, their arms entwined, their voices raised suddenly to join Dimitri's song, as though, after all, this moment they had feared all winter long held some secret joy for them only now remembered … good-bye … and beside us old Emmanuele Manglis replacing his black cap and puffing out his whiskers and blowing his nose rather loudly into a red handkerchief … and the thin young boy called Petros, who had swaggered and boasted through the weeks preceding Easter, suddenly jerking up behind the straining figure of Dimitri to wave a desperate handkerchief … 'Mama! Good-bye, Mama! …' and the *Sevasti* sweeping in and past with a foam of white at her lean crimson bow, and crippled Dionyssos hanging in the rigging bawling a lewd parody of the shopping announcements he had called through the long winter …

Good-bye … *kaló taxethi* … good journey … Day after day through the ten days immediately following Easter the diving boats skimmed on the golden evening seas in groups of five, of ten, of twelve, of fifteen, bound for the African beds, with the dinghies rowing out from the long pier where the women stood weeping and the flags snapped in the wind and the church bells pealed … *Kaló taxethi* …

Saklarades, Captain Miches, Fotes, Costas Manglis, Dionyssos, American Mike, Mikailis the *colazáris* and Mikailis the *ferneze,* old Dimitri and young Petros … the wild ones, the crazy ones, the *pallikaria* …

The truth and the meaning of the little island lay here, in these men. Year after year this same scene was repeated, signalling the beginning of another unique and incredible human adventure. And year after year it passed unnoticed. There are so many celluloid braveries to preoccupy the world after all, and comic strips of spacemen, and every year the jets fly faster and the bombs make louder bangs and football players fetch a higher price. And every year the boats go out from Kalymnos …

Every evening after the dinghies had taken the last of the stragglers out we would go back to the house and from the balcony watch the boats sailing out into the twilight gulf. For all the harbour was below us, and the open sea as far as Point Cali. I think our figures must have been sharply defined on that spindly balcony against the pale lime-washed wall, because often the last thing we would hear, drifting very faint and sad across the water, were the names of Martin and Shane.

'O Martis! Say!' they would call from the rigging. Very faint, very sad, it would drift to us. The talismanic words. The golden children of the new world.

Sometimes we would bring back with us the regulars who appeared on the pier every evening: Georgios, the sponge merchant with the guilty conscience, old Leonidas the cake seller, *Capitano* Anthonis, Emmanuele Manglis, a few others who knew the deep meaning of the going away of the boats. And Yanni, of course, a little angry and humiliated, and jealous of our obvious emotion.

'Yes,' he would say bitterly, 'and when I went off to the war, Charmian, there was nobody in the world to wave me good-bye!' Or, with a slight experimental derision, 'No wonder the women are weeping; half of them will starve through the summer to pay off the winter's gambling and drinking!' And finally, in a last pathetic attempt to win us back, he would fabricate some story in which he had been prevented from becoming a diver only by Polymnea's threats of suicide.

But for once his appeals for sympathy and admiration were quite lost on us. We would stand in a row along the balcony, the old men and George and I, blowing our noses hard and prodding our knuckles at specks of dust in our eyes, while out by the lighthouse the schooners weighed anchor and slowly, heavily, ceremoniously made their three wide formal circles of the harbour. The rigging would be black and wriggling with the divers clinging to it, and the slim brilliant working boats would leap after them like puppies, making a dozen extravagant circles for every one of the mother ship.

From the two churches specifically devoted to the interests of the seamen, Saint Stephanos and Saint Nikolas, the bells would rock and ring a wild protestation of good faith — the divers had been most devout the last few days, and there had been a great many last-minute, or at least eleventh-hour, prayers and promises and propitiations, candles and repentances for the two saints to heed. And beating on the bell-beaten evening every window on every hill would be agitated with the flutter of handkerchiefs and scarves and tablecloths. The wild bells would ring and the windows and balconies fume and flap their colours until the boats were only dull freckles on the milled yellow cliffs of Pserimos. And when you blinked your eyes they were gone.

Then we would make a count of the boats still left in the harbour — forty boats ... thirty ... fifteen ... ten ... and after each such tally I would observe the old men glancing furtively over towards the Klonaris coffee-house, where through the small square window you could see the black cap and slumped shoulders and the narrow neck of an *ouzo* bottle. Apart from *him* the coffee-house was always empty at this hour, and he always sat with his back to the window.

'Coffee, Manolaichi?' old Anthonis would say, giving the name the affectionate diminutive that made it sould like a child wheedling for favours.

'Hrrmp!' Emmanuele Manglis would grunt, tugging angrily at his moustache. 'Coffee, yes — but not there.'

'Think how he feels now. It would be a kindness ...'

'And be cursed for your trouble!'

'That? It's only the pain speaking in him. I understand it.'

'He's not a good man, Anthonis. I don't care for him.'

And Anthonis would smile his sweet, sad smile. 'Only God knows, Manoli, how good he is or bad.' And beneath his arm he would tuck the heavy wooden box of cigarettes with the little ships painted on the lid, and he would bid us all good night and go downstairs. Crossing the *plateia* he loooked very small and very old, and the big box was a cruel weight, tilting his body over to one side.

'Hrrmp!' Manglis would grunt again, more violently. 'I'd better go after him, I suppose. I have a stronger head for curses than he has. The trouble with him is that he's a Christian. If he didn't think first of charity and love he'd see that it's no kindness at all for two old crocks like us to go in there and sit with *him*. Not now. After all,' he would add grimly, looking after the small, bent, shuffling figure in the shabby coat, 'Anthonis was once a captain too.'

We never really did piece together the full story of the man who sat in the Klonaris coffee-house every evening. I suppose we could have easily enough, but there was too much of privacy that had to be intruded on. He was a sponge captain, a man of late middle-age with one good fast boat now buoyed out from the breakwater with those boats of the fleet which had not yet left for Africa. But where all the other boats were brave in new paint and clean white rigging and new Greek flags that wives and sisters had stitched, his was grey and stained and peeling from the winter cruise, and its rust-streaked weather cloths hung in torn shreds from dirty ropes. The diving ladder was lashed up, the wire propeller cages lay rusting and neglected on the unscrubbed deck, and the deck itself was bare of the neat white coils of hose, the racked oil drums, the neatly folded diving suits, the piled copper helmets that gave each of the other boats its air of purpose and meaning.

We had seen the boat come in months before from its winter cruise. American Mike had sailed in her as engineer but he was always rather taciturn about the trip. It hadn't been particularly successful, and the young diver Panorimides had been crippled on his first cruise. We used to see the captain frequently around the coffee-houses, but somehow we never made friends with him. He seemed a surly man and he was involved almost every day in squabbles with his divers and crew about money due to them. Once or twice the squabbles ended in real brawls. American Mike, as I say, was not very communicative, which was surprising enough in so friendly and loquacious a man, but it was clear that it had not been a particularly happy trip. In any event Mike signed up with another captain for the summer cruise, and most of the divers did too.

Whether it was because of the boy being crippled, or the poor harvest of sponges, or a general dissatisfaction among the men who had sailed with him, or the disputes about money, or the man's own sullen and bitter nature, or whether it was merely the accumulation of many little unpleasantnesses that had somehow gathered into a little cloud of evil that clung to him — where the truth was to be found in all these things nobody could or would say. But within a couple of months people were avoiding him, and when he applied to the bank for the advance to fit out his boat for the summer cruise the bank refused him. (American Mike said he had asked for too much money and refused to accept the smaller amount which the bank offered, and it might have been as simple as that.)

At first he didn't seem to realise that the bank's rejection would be final, or perhaps he stubbornly refused to believe it, because he blustered and bullied as much as ever and he signed up a few divers — none of the good ones — and he talked loudly about the killing he was going to make in summer off

190

the Benghazi beds. Even when all the other boats were sailed round to Lavassi for fitting out he didn't seem to mind much. When he wasn't sitting under the salt tree drinking coffee or boasting or quarrelling he was aboard his own boat, busy at something or other.

It was only when the banks began to issue their advances and the other captains were flashing great rolls of banknotes about that he began to look a little uneasy.

This was a brisk, businesslike time in the town, and the captains were in and out of the shops all day, ordering salt and flour and macaroni and new ropes and sidelights and deadeyes and tackle, and the bakehouses were beginning on the *galetis*. Every day the captains were backward and forward between Lavassi and the harbourmaster's office with passports and fresh lists or sitting in groups at coffee checking names and papers.

It was about this time that the divers who had signed on with him began to show signs of restlessness. When were they going to be paid their advances? If it came to that, when would the boat get away if fitting out hadn't even begun? For a week or so he held them on promises, but there was a desperate look in his eyes now as he walked every morning from the salt tree to the bank. After ten minutes he'd come back again, his shoulders very straight and his cap at a jaunty angle, but his face was angry and puzzled and his confident talk of expecting the advance to come through tomorrow wouldn't have deceived anybody.

Within a week the divers had all signed on in other boats. After that he didn't go to the bank any more. There was no point in getting an advance if he couldn't get divers to sail with him.

Now he would sit all day under the salt tree, drinking coffee or *ouzo*, never speaking to anybody, and he never went near his own boat except sometimes at night when the *plateia* was deserted. From our balcony we could see the glow of his cigarette bobbing about and hear him muttering and cursing in the darkness.

It was when the boats began to leave that he moved inside the Klonaris coffee-house. He always sat with his back to the window, drinking *ouzo*.

Old Anthonis was the only one who ever seemed to have a true pity for him. I often found myself wondering whether it was more than the old cigarette seller's natural sweetness and Christian charity. Was this the way it had happened to him too? Was this the point where a man turned down that long, pitted incline that led to the cigarette box or the *ballaixi bag*? As Emmanuele Manglis had pointed out, Anthonis had been a captain too.

In any case it was old Anthonis who would go every evening and sit with his morose, ungrateful companion and drink a glass of something for company and talk a bit, mostly to himself. And old Emmanuele would shake his head and follow after, lurching painfully on his stick across the *plateia* with his bad leg trailing and his hip jutting at a grotesque angle, and his set shoulders expressing complete disapproval of the whole thing.

On the whole I think he had the right of it, and the presence of the two old men at that outcast table was a mistake, however charitably intended. If they had not been there perhaps the outcast could have told himself that it was nothing after all. What was one season? Next season it would be easy enough to get the advance, and then he could easily recoup his losses. Hadn't he always said he wanted a few months off, a rest from it for a while? Everyone had bad luck at some time or other, and he was a good seaman, everyone in the port knew that.

One evening I went over to the coffee-house twenty minutes or so after Anthonis had left our house — I had forgotten to buy cigarettes. The bells were still ringing the boats out, and they were sitting together at the corner table in the otherwise empty room: the two sad, kind old men and the surly half-drunken captain. It shocked me to see how much his face had changed; the face that had been so quick with pride and violence and anger now seemed no more than a mirror reflecting the two faces across the table. Or perhaps they were the mirror, and the captain had only just recognised that he was looking at himself. In any case he looked old too.

17

There was an unaccustomed silence in Skeftarios' bleak bare room and a new sort of people around the checked tablecloths — the clerks from the banks and the officials from the customs house and the post office and bands of quiet fishermen who had come down from Piraeus and New Phaleron to net the strait with flaring carbide lamps mounted on the prows of their little *gri-gri* boats. Their boats were very small moored at the market end of the harbour. The main harbour was empty — abandoned to the bobbing floats and buoys the sponge fleet had left behind at its moorings.

We hated it all: the emptiness, the silence, the yawning hollows that those fifteen hundred warm, wild men had left in the life of the town. And then a letter came from our publisher in New York to say that the novel had been accepted. It would be published in the autumn.

'It's all right!' we assured each other again and again, both of us suddenly sick with relief. 'It came off after all. It's all right!'

What would we do now? We had added the publisher's advance to what money we still had left and were sitting once more over sheets of scrawled and scratched-out figures. A second golden untouched year stretched away ahead of the first.

'*Do?* We'll have a drink!' said George, whose convivial impulses are inclined to be alcoholic. 'In fact, we'll have several. Have a party.'

Of course we'd have a party. But after the party, what would we do then? We had done what we came to Kalymnos to do — we had earned ourselves a slice of time. Now we could transfer ourselves to one of the islands that we used to dream about — Mykonos maybe, or Santorini, or Hydra, or Spetsai. We could send for our books and pictures and establish a proper working base.

'Ye-es,' said George a little doubtfully. 'I suppose we'll have to think about it, won't we?'

Martin, entering at this moment with two crabs in a hat, said: 'What will we have to think about?'

'Where we'll go when we leave Kalymnos.'

'But, Mum! Dad!' His face buckled. 'We can't leave Kalymnos yet! We can't! Just when Georgouli's mother has made a coffee-house at the *therma* and Georgouli's going to row me there every day in a boat, and Apostoli is making me a mask for underwater swimming, and Angela says we can go and stay in her summer house whenever we like. And, Mum, it's *summer*! There are *sika* and *piponia* and —'

'And *staphilia* and *fronkosika* …' George chanted the ending of the litany of summer fruits with him. 'Well, don't worry about it now, Marty. It's only something to think about. We won't do anything immediately.'

'And there's my school,' said Martin doggedly.

'Don't worry, Marty. We wouldn't dream of doing anything before school finishes for the year.'

After he had gone, still not entirely reassured, to find Apostoli, I said, 'It *would* be silly to take them away before the end of the school year, wouldn't it? And then the beach here is so marvellous for them. So safe.' I felt inexplicably relieved.

'And it wouldn't be bad to take things a little more easily ourselves for a few months,' George said luxuriously. 'Swim and fish and catch up on some reading. Why,' he added daringly, 'I might even learn Greek.'

'Yes, and when we go there are all those bags to be packed again.'

'And you'll have to find another Sevasti …'

Another Sevasti! What would we do without Sevasti? And what would Sevasti do without those few extra *drachmae* each month? And Yanni's migration papers were not yet finalised. We ought to wait until that was settled and Yanni was ready to leave for Australia.

'And anyway,' said George, 'I'd rather like to be around when the boats come back. I like those wild bastards.'

And so do I. Fotes and Saklarades of the ham hands, young Captain Charlie, Mikailis the *colazáris* and Mikailis the *ferneze,* American Mike … they *had* to come back safely, all of them. And it would be good to be there on the wharf to say 'Welcome home!'

'All right then. We'll stay until the boats come back. Everyone,' I added hopefully, 'says it is absolute heaven in summer.'

George grinned. 'We'll save the lotus for next year. This year let's eat prickly pear like all our friends.'

'It's called *frankosika*.'

'*Sika, piponia, staphilia, frankosika* ...'

It was Shane who had the last word. 'When you go away from Kalymnos, Mummie, will you leave me two of *your* dresses?' She pronounces it *th*resses, in a strong Greek accent.

'Why, love?'

'Well, it's all right now while I'm little, but Heleni's mummie is very poor and I don't think she'd be able to buy me dresses when I'm big. Two of yours will do for when I grow.'

'You won't be coming with us then?'

'Oh, no!' Shane was wide-eyed at the thought. 'I've asked Heleni's mother. She says it will be quite all right. I can move into their house whenever I like.'

18

It is the last day of the school year — the day the children are to deliver publicly the poems they have been rehearsing gravely for the past three weeks — and we, with all the other parents, grandparents, aunts, uncles, brothers, sisters and cousins of the two hundred children who attend the Black School, present ourselves as instructed at eight o'clock on this summer morning already milky with heat.

It seems an unreasonable hour to begin speech-day proceedings even here, where time seems to be much more malleable than it is in the Western countries. The headmaster seems to be conscious of this and points out earnestly that as every one of the two hundred children has a poem to say, besides the songs and dances in which everyone will take part, it is most necessary to make an early start.

Kyria I-Heraklia, who has guided Martin and Shane through their first Greek classes, ushers us to seats on a wooden form behind a large desk covered with oilcloth. She makes a short, dignified speech to excuse the poverty of the school. An earnest woman in her early forties, she has for this day abandoned her customary dress of black gathered skirt, tightly buttoned bodice and severe black coif, and is almost unrecognisable in a shiny figured satin dress that shows the stiff ribs and knotted lacing of her corsets. I have never seen her head bare before. It is surprising somehow to see that there are beautiful faded streaks of red among the crimped grey.

Her speech is received with cheers and applause by the children, to whom poverty has only a dramatic meaning, and with sighs and apologetic head-shaking by the parents and relatives who now crowd into the schoolroom doorway, swarm over the chipped desks ranged tightly against the wall or perch high on the window ledges.

We move along the wooden form to make room for some of them, but they shake their heads shyly. Evidently we are the guests of honour and must sit solitary and splendid.

Looking around at the women in their patched prints and at the men, shy and ill at ease in shirts buttoned to the throat and shiny jackets that show the marks of the charcoal iron, I realise again what a handsome people this is. It is not a matter of feature alone, although their features are usually strong and definite and they almost always have clear skins, fine eyes and rich hair. Perhaps they are so impressive as a people because their normal expression — I realise this as I look around the crowded schoolroom — is one of quiet dignity. And I realise too that although I have seen these faces show grief, anger, bewilderment, laughter, pride, passion and sometimes resignation, what gives the faces a nobility almost unnatural in our age is the complete absence of resentment and pettishness, or those tell-tale lines that mark the frustration of little egos. Thinking of the pallid faces and apathetic eyes descending into the costive bowels of the early morning tube stations at this very hour in London, I find myself wondering if frustration is one of the inevitable by-products of sophistication. Cities, I think, give a sense of insignificance and helplessness in the same way as they give a sense of assurance that trains will run and postmen will call and the garbage will be taken away. But everything becomes the sum of its own assurance, the mass of its moving tide. It is the tide alone that retains purpose and meaning; its components are no more than cells splitting and dividing, their differences one from another of no importance, their dignity as free souls lost, even to themselves. Only the tide that moves them, and in which they move, retains its meaning.

These grave faces packed into the poor little schoolroom could only grow from a life where life's values are more simply and more clearly defined — birth and copulation and death, mysteries that are still grave and terrible, that are the simple recognition of immediate moments, never things of retrospect, moments that are to be grasped and poured out again, given back in song and dance and the shared communion of wine. Wine is still a mystic rite, filled with the power and presence of old and powerful gods. Here bread is still the staff of life, a well of sweet water is more than jewels, a tree is shade, a piece of fertile ground is earth that will grow food, and hands are still marvellous creative instruments that can take the raw, rough stuff of rock and soil and water and make from it warmth and comfort, and beauty too. Perhaps there is neither time nor room for the trivial emotions that lay the marks of disfigurement on the city face, not here in lives where joy and sorrow are scaled to the mountains and the wind and the eternal beat of the sea.

(We had been walking back from the market two days before, keeping to the pavement and the shade of the salt trees, for even at nine o'clock in the morning the sun bit fiercely. There were isolated groups of men at the cafe tables — men without work, old men who no longer cared, young men killing time until their permits came to take them to Australia, family men who still hoped. All through the dazzle and the dapple of the sun and shade the silk tassels of the *kombollois* flashed like humming birds and the beads clicked their idle, repetitious rhythms.

A woman with a basket of market fruits walked without haste near the railings by the sea. Far behind her the boy from the post office ran a few jerky steps, hesitated and ran forward again. He was holding a folded yellow slip in his stiffly extended hand, as if it was something he had to get rid of but could not shake from his fingers.

Afterwards it seemed that all the men from the coffee tables must have been running before the boy even caught up with the woman, because I cannot remember him handing her the yellow slip of paper. And when she screamed, it was a sound that came from the middle of a cluster of people, and there were women running down from the alleys and the side streets. Some potatoes and onions were rolling among all the scuffling feet, and a wheel of bread bowled along like a child's hoop a little way down the *plateia*, before it spun a crazy circle and fell flat.

The men went back to the coffee tables slowly, holding their caps in their hands and crossing themselves. The woman went away with the other women leading her. She had the yellow slip of paper clutched tightly against her chest. Her white scarf had slipped off and her hair had come unfastened. It was very long and dark, and she kept tossing her head so that her hair lashed backward and forward across her face. When they reached the pavement she began to scream again, but the other women were packed tightly around her and you could only see the strands of black hair lashing, lashing, lashing, as if the hair itself were screaming.

There was no need to ask what had happened. We had seen it all before, three times already since the boats had left, and we would see it again. Another diver had been lost off Africa.

Two men picked up the spilled onions and potatoes and the disc of bread and arranged them carefully. Then they called a boy and sent him off with them.

The wide road was still and shimmering and empty again, and the coloured silk tassels were flicking restlessly in the shade beneath the salt trees. It was at least an hour before the passing bell began to toll.)

In the schoolroom the children are obviously wearing their very best clothes. Most of the little boys have their heads freshly shaven. 'The egg-shaped ones,' Martin used to call them. Now he is as egg-shaped as they are, except that his round, bumpy skull — looking startlingly large and fragile above the small, patched, peeling face — is shadowed faintly yellow instead of the blue-black of the other boys'. He wears the same clothes as they — clean shorts, washed and pressed many times into a faded softness, a clean white shirt and blue and white canvas sneakers. Nearly all the boys are wearing shoes today. Some even have socks.

The little girls are frizzed and curled like dolls, and they wear enormous stiff bows perched in their hair like gaudy butterflies. You can tell quite easily which of them have relatives in America, because the second-hand American cotton dresses sent in clothing parcels from their more fortunate cousins and now primped up with extra bows, brooches, necklaces, medallions and plastic crosses are of better material and smarter cut. For Shane the nuns at Argos have woven a dress of heavy white cotton embroidered with bands of blue. She would prefer red satin or purple taffeta fastened with a brooch of glass emeralds, but on the whole she is quite pleased with herself. This is the first new dress she has had since we left London. Every few minutes Sevasti pushes her way through the crush to where the children are herded at the far end of the room to comb Shane's hair or adjust her sash. I have the feeling that she secretly wishes I had made rather more display of my only daughter.

The schoolroom is large — no nice, easily handleable groups here — the paintwork is peeling, the prevalent atmosphere is of a painful scrimping to make the poverty of the place less manifest. It is sparsely decorated — the usual brightly tinted portraits of King Paul and Queen Frederika, a lithograph of the Greek heroine Boubalina in imperious profile, with a smaller inset showing her in action, directing artillery fire against the Turks, a hand-drawn and coloured multiplication chart using bright bunches of cherries as counting symbols, and a very large and complicated diagram that depicts the seasons and the agricultural year. This is interesting not only for the effortless, primitive charm of the drawing (one of the teachers had done it in her spare time, I was told) but also for the fact that not a single piece of mechanised equipment is shown. There is nothing but the age-old components of agriculture in Greece: the man, the mule, the sickle, the circular threshing floor. Coifed women winnow with flat trays, and the chaff blows away on the wind.

The far end of the room opens out on to a little chapel, very Byzantine in character if not in truth, and especially pretty for the children, with much lace and gilt and flowers. One is not surprised to learn that the chapel rests on the foundations of an ancient Temple of Artemis — Artemis the Stranger.

By nine o'clock the crowd at last has settled, and the poems begin amid shushings, giggles, howling babies and spurts of conversation abruptly curtailed.

Each child in turn climbs onto an improvised platform which began inviolate but which is now also seating space for parents and relatives and a crawling area for baby brothers and sisters. The girls curtsy, the boys bow or salute, and one after another rattle through their *peemas*, which are delivered loud and fast and with a curious set of accompanying gestures, stiff and stylised. The girls' poems concern the Virgin, the gentler saints, flowers, donkeys, butterflies, modesty, cheerfulness, obedience, hard work. The boys' are concerned with derring-do, blood, battle heroes and the massacre of Turks.

Martin and Shane appear early in the programme. Martin wears a red *evzone* cap, brandishes a wooden sword and declaims in perfect Greek on the joys of being a guerrilla fighter in the mountains. Shane, in loud deadpan, declares her ambition to be a great help to me in the kitchen. Her hand makes stiff embracing gestures all the while. I take this to denote aspiration. They are both applauded good-naturedly and vigorously, and everyone turns to beam at the proud parents. We *are* proud, and I'm sure we are beaming too.

It is almost midday by the time the poems are through, and while the smaller girls perform circular linked dances to an accompanying song about the season, all parents are herded off to the headmaster's office to receive the school reports.

In England they always came through the post with a stern mimeographed injunction that they were on no account to be shown to or discussed with the children. Here they are presented ceremonially — large, ornately decorated documents that startled George for a moment because they looked exactly like the command of the Earl Marshal of England to attend the coronation of Queen Elizabeth the Second. I suppose one *is* meant to frame them, and after all they would look very pretty, since they are covered with the beautiful pastel-coloured Greek stamps that depict the Colossus of Rhodes, the Charioteer of Delphi and the heads of both Pericles and the Medusa.

Both our certificates bear the maximum mark, ten. I suspect this is less a true recording of the scholastic prowess of our children than a compliment to us as foreigners and a sign of *Kyria I-Heraklia's* blatant favouritism. But what a splendid, proud, extravagant, exciting document it is! Less a report than a diploma ... and if one is dubious that two foreign children could not only master a totally strange and new language in the space of a few months, but also become perfectly proficient in the reading and writing of it, one cannot begrudge them their diplomas.

One feels that they have earned some very special mark of recognition for all the bad food they have eaten, for the rough voyages on smelly caiques, for the times they've been cold and lonely and uncomfortable and homesick, for those early panics when life itself must have seemed to be disintegrating into fear and desolation, for the first time Martin won a fight and all the times he didn't — for all the tremendous effort of readjustment that had led to this proud moment in the headmaster's office. I would give them a diploma too. And perhaps, after all *that* is what those absurdly high marks mean.

At this point there is a great deal of shaking hands, of mutual wishes for happiness and prosperity. George makes a stumbling and completely ungrammatical speech in which he thanks all the teachers for their interest in the children and their help in making them literate in Greek. The headmaster responds with a fluent and beautifully grammatical speech thanking us for honouring the school and assuring us of the excellence of the children's scholarship and their undoubted promise of becoming as worthy, as noble, as clever as their parents. Shane, hideously embarrassed by her father's lamentable Greek, attempts to break it all up by curtsying quickly to each teacher and kissing their hands — she is quick to pick up all the extravagances of foreign

203

ways — but this self-conscious performance suddenly collapses into real hugs of affection. Martin, pink with pride, shakes hands roundly with everyone, the precious report clutched to his shirt-front.

We walk down through the twisting coloured alleys to the wide waterfront and the beating blue sea, greeting and being greeted by other parents and their children. Through the whole town runs a fever of excitement and congratulation and of achievement. How important it is that the little ones have survived another year of education! How clever they will all be! This morning all the future unfolds upon dawns as red as apples, a future in which each child is transformed by the mysterious alchemy of education into one of the feared and respected *plusius* — the wealthy. And there are shoes and overcoats and beds with mattresses and dowries of millions of *drachmae* for the accomplished, educated sisters and warm inviolable corners for the old people, and meals come three times a day at the clap of a hand, with an elegant thimble of *strega* to accompany the preserves.

It is with high, singing hearts that we give one another the loveliest of Greek greetings, 'And another year!'

One way and another it takes us quite a long time to get along the waterfront to the spindly yellow house we have come to call home.

19

Summer holidays! The school reports, rather thumbed now by all the neighbours, have been carefully put away. The great earthenware bowl on the table is piled with melons and grapes and figs and pears — and tomatoes as well, because the colours are nice. The children have been given five *drachmae* each as an end-of-school treat. For five *drachmae* they can buy twenty-five of the tiny twenty-*lepta* cones, and they are pelting along the *plateia* after the ice-cream cart with a dozen of their friends. The ice-cream is horrid stuff, rather like a frozen, lumpy custard in which the cornflour wasn't cooked long enough, and it's made by teenage boys who sit in the gutters twirling the long cylindrical cans around in tubs of ice. But the ice-cream is worthwhile for the spectacle of the carts that carry it — gorgeous wooden chariots painted blue and yellow and scarlet and white, with bands of little flowers on the plywood panels, and each spoke of the thick wheels painted in a different colour. Martin and Shane obviously get more pleasure from the purchase of one of these tiny cones, no larger than a child's finger, than they ever did from the rainbow bricks with chocolate sauce of London. Perhaps they have just forgotten …

London, and the summer holidays of London, seem so much more than two or three thousand miles away. This was the time when I would have been putting away all my own work and plans to concentrate on the least desperate measures for keeping the children amused and healthy in the three months of summer holidays — the time of tension and nightmare and tight controls.

Sitting here on the balcony above the harbour I found myself recalling ridiculous and terrifying things: the lumps of dough I would give them to play with in the kitchen while I scurried and scamped through the housework to try to gain an hour or two when I could walk them through the park before it was time to do the marketing and prepare their luncheon. And those asphalted playing areas and the sooty leaves that drifted sadly over them, and the concrete pits of dirty grey sand ... the fretful hours of manoeuvring through snarling city traffic to get to the tamed green spaces of Richmond Park, where for an hour or so they might paddle and run and climb the trees, and even feed the deer if the park keepers were not looking. And through it all I would be miserably conscious that beds were unmade and shopping undone and saucepans probably burned dry. And there was the two weeks' planned holiday by the sea, by the cold, grey opacity of that sea that sighed against the damp, dark shingle — the two weeks that always stretched to four weeks, or six, or eight, while bills mounted higher and higher and George somehow managed alone in London because he wouldn't allow the children to be cooped up for the summer in a flat on the Bayswater Road. It is strange and in its way triumphant to realise that in Greece we have lived this year, the four of us, on what it cost last year for holidays alone!

Yet it is still a little difficult to realise that now nothing is expected of me, no special plans, no extra effort, no resolutions about keeping control and smiling through the next three months. For the children it has become part of an endless seaside holiday, and I need not concern myself much more than to round them up for meals and bedtime. And George, when his morning's work is finished, can sit and drink his wine in the sun with his long legs stretched out on the second chair always provided for just that purpose.

I can see him down below me now drawing maps and diagrams. And in the branches of the tree above the table an octopus is drying, grey and flat, and another is hanging in the tree beyond, and another beyond that. It is so utterly Kalymnian. All the way down the street the octopi hang like a flat grey fringe, tasselled and tentacled, marking off the golden edge of the morning.

'Are you going to swim?' I call. I still feel that it is slightly immoral to be so casual about the blue and heavenly Aegean and must remind myself that we have both completed our morning's work and there is no reason on earth why we should *not* swim.

Old habits are hard to shake off: I cannot yet say *'Then pirasi'* or *'avrio'* quite casually. And I still feel a slight unease to see George actually relaxing. Subconsciously my feet still twitch occasionally, remembering the treadmill.

George lifts his *retzina* glass to the window in a formal toast, winks conspiratorially and goes down the wide street in search of the children.

There is a loaf of fresh black bread and a thick slab of *graviera*, the Cretan cheese, and a big watermelon to eat on the rocks, and there are the swimming things in a big basket.

'Today's the day,' says Martin importantly, 'when Apostoli and Georgouli show me how to dive with the stone. We'll probably get a few sponges for you, I expect.'

'And since the day is very hot and there's no wind,' says Sevasti, putting aside her brooms and brushes with an air of decision, 'there's no reason why I shouldn't come too.'

'What about the grippe?' says George warningly.

'Bah!' snorts Sevasti.

By the time we have skirted the harbour and taken the first easy climb on the cliff road that leads towards the *therma* we have become a sizeable party of three adults and a dozen children.

Just beyond the church of Saint Nikolas Yanni is working, banging up the supports for a balcony. His work is rough and vigorous, and his tools are scattered all over the road. He is stripped to the waist and glossy with sweat.

'Where are you going? I thought you were working.'

'It's too wonderful a day. We decided we'd swim.'

'Let's go.'

'But your work, Yanni!'

'*This?* Bah! Five minutes I could finish it in, one-hand kneeling!'

Along the ruined parapet beside the house a group of old women are perched, cutting old clothing into long strips that will later be woven into rag rugs. They are black and white among the bright rag streamers festooned from the parapet, hooded and hooked like birds, and like birds their eyes are bright and watchful and knowing.

'Ah, Yanni has a holiday today then,' one of them cackles, and another answers her, 'No, no. He is a rich man, this Yanni. It doesn't matter whether he works or not. Haven't you seen the new dresses his wife and children are always getting these days?'

The sarcasm is heavy and pointed, and apart from a muttered *'Gorgonas!'* Yanni does not deign — or dare — to reply to them. He has forgotten, however, that Sevasti is one of the party, and with great relish she takes up where the women on the parapet have left off. Even when we are far past the slaughterhouse, climbing a rutted track pitched among the parched rocks between heaven and sea, the two of them are still needling each other. The war of the sexes is unending.

Now the track dips down to a narrow blue inlet studded with tiny rocky islets and fringed with pebbles. The children begin to run, but as the adult party breasts the rise all the islets writhe and fly apart as fifty naked youths dive for cover into the sea. It seems we must go farther yet, skirting the inlet — Sevasti and I with our eyes modestly averted, for after the first show of reticence (and perhaps we were thought to be the police) the policy has changed. Now the youths are all clambering about the rocks or posing in a sort of young defiant arrogance in their nakedness. And so we cross the Italian bridge where the parapets have almost crumbled away and follow the trail that rises again to the new tumble of rocks and rubble that enshrine the *therma*.

The hot springs — the finest medicinal springs in Greece, according to some — bubble up under the ochre cliffs in an area littered with the debris of the occasional and sporadic blasting carried out from time to time at the whim of some mayor who has decided to make the place a tourist attraction. These earlier attempts at civic progress had all been abandoned through lack of funds or lack of interest or the termination of a period of office or the ending of a need to canvass votes, or perhaps sheer weight of the work to be done before any tourist in his right senses could be cajoled into getting that far. Anyone sick enough to need the hot springs would surely be intimidated by the long, rough trail from the town. No car could travel that track, and there is no other approach except from the sea.

There is a retaining wall by the sea, and a small jetty, but there was some funny business, we are told, about the contract for this construction, and both the retaining wall and jetty failed to give much resistance to the first heavy seas and are now in a state as sad and ruinous as everything else. There is talk now of rebuilding it all, and a new road out has actually been begun, but in the stillness of death it is hard to believe in resurrection.

In the meantime the sick of the island use the springs in summer. Georgouli's mother sees a few extra *drachmae* in this and by dint of Herculean labour has built a little summer shelter of boughs and whitewashed poles. Here she serves coffee and drinks to sufferers after their baths. She has cleaned out the pavilion too, and the concrete tubs where the hot waters circulate from the inside of the earth. A monumental task this, like cleaning the Augean stables, for all the winter and for many winters past the building has been used as a public lavatory. (It is one of the more disconcerting thoughts about Greece that any empty building with four walls and a door is inevitably used as a public lavatory, even if it stands alone on a rocky mountain miles from anywhere!)

Ladies in coloured petticoats scuttle like queer, bright-shelled beach crabs into the pavilion as we pass, and Georgouli's mother calls a shrill injunction to be sure and stop for coffee on our way back. Georgouli waits behind to beg bread and oil from her for all the children. Sevasti resolves again to take the course of hot baths for her rheumatism. Yanni tells of more marvellous cures.

We tramp on, up the cliff path and down again on the other side. Here is a curve of bone-grey pebbles, a cave, a fig tree for shade, a wide, flat vermilion rock for sunbathing. The children, stripped to cotton briefs, are diving in the water before we get there. Martin and Shane hold their noses and simply jump, but the water here is forty feet deep at the edge of the rocks, and in a moment they are following the bigger children out to where the water's blue is turning violet — Shane paddling furiously like a young puppy, and Martin with his arms at last triumphantly out of the water in a weird sort of lolloping crawl. They are both fifty yards out to sea by the time we reach the shore. It is wonderful to think you can turn your back on them and know they are safe.

Yanni disappears behind the rocks on our left. Sevasti bobs down discreetly behind the fig tree on our right. In this formation we shall swim. We shall be in the centre, the family party; Yanni will swim fifty yards to our left, Sevasti fifty yards to our right. So the sex distinctions will be maintained, modesty preserved, and the traditions of Kalymnos upheld.

Sevasti creeps from behind her tree, her old red shift gathered up like an ancient *chiton*, her head still carelessly coifed in white muslin. Yanni, wearing only his white underpants, climbs away up the cliff on our left, holds himself rigid against the sky for a moment and dives like a brown arrow into the water. Sevasti slides in breast on. Undisturbed by so much as a bubble, the sea closes around her. She sails away sedately. Neither of them has glanced at the other or at us. Yanni is on the high rock again and hurtling down like Icarus falling from heaven. Sevasti is out behind the children, breaststroking gently in the direction of Kos, making so little disturbance of the water that her white headscarf is mirrored exactly in reflection. She is a twin-headed image imprinted upon the deep blue of the sea.

We pull the last tape and adjust the last buckle, and George follows me in that long, green, gasping plunge back into the most magical of all the elements.

And now we are transformed. Our bodies, freed of their weight, float and flow in the greenish-gold, the goldish-green, the sun-dapple, the cavernous shadows. Our hair streams in the seashine, our bodies, following each other, are wet brown scrawls wavering over the weeds and the sand. We are forced to the sun-sparkling, dancing surface only by the gulping need of our gill-less bodies, and we float there gasping. But this too is wonderful — to bathe in both elements at once — the warm air and the cold sea, with little dizzy currents of warmth lapping our legs and flowing on. There is a slow soft swell coming in from the southward, and we rock and rock under that great inverted bowl of blue. Surely it must tip a little to let us see what is on the other side, there at the sharp rim of things where the oyster gap between sea and sky opens up at dawn? The soaring stones of the old baked mountains peak and fall gently along miles of angled light and out of the world of perspective and rules. Kos heaves ponderously in the corner of my vision. There is an albatross in the sky, and in my ears the low, exultant murmur of immense watery wheels turning.

There is a blue boat with a tan sail dipping and drifting in towards the rock shelf of the shore. I can see Sevasti bobbing and bending about the ledges far down the cove, gathering shellfish in her wet red skirt. George is hauling himself up the weeded rock to join Yanni, who is squatting over a shiny purple pile of sea urchins.

The boat with the tan sail has come in close. Ropes are trailing from the side, and the children are dragging it in. They seem so small and bright and shining and far away, small singing scraps of flesh and colour in the great grave cadences of sunlight.

'Come! Come!' Their calls drift across the water. 'Martin! Martin! Come and sail in the boat! Come!'

Martin is standing by himself on the pebbles in front of the cave. One hand still loosely holds a long glistening trail of dark kelp. One foot still lingers in the sea. His head is high, his face dazed, curiously arrested.

'*Martin!*' they call again, and he turns his head slowly towards the boat and the other children. Slowly he goes towards them, almost reluctantly, the kelp trailing forgotten from his hand, looking back over his shoulder as he goes, as though he is watching for something … or listening …

And now they are calling me. 'Come! Come!' they cry across the water. 'Come and sail!' George is holding the boat. They are all scrambling over the gunwhales, beneath the slow, warm slap of the tan sail. 'Come!'

Not yet … not for a moment. If I stay for a moment, only a moment, perhaps I might hear it too — that one rare mermaid, singing.